Joy to the world! the Lord is come;
Let earth receive her King;
Let every heart prepare Him room,
And heav'n and nature sing.

COME...
AND
BEHOLD
HIM!

An Invitation to
Christmas Worship

JACK HAYFORD

MULTNOMAH BOOKS • SISTERS, OREGON

COME AND BEHOLD HIM
published by Multnomah Publishers, Inc.

© 1995 by David C. Needham

International Standard Book Number 0-88070-738-0
Special FCP Edition 1-893065-56-1

Cover illustration *The Nativity* by Gustave Doré
Cover design by Kirk DouPonce

Printed in the United States of America

Most Scripture quotations are from.
The New Revised Standard Version Bible
© 1989 Division of Christian Education of the National Council
of the Churches of Christ in the United States of America

Scripture quotations marked NIV are from the Holy Bible,
New International Version,
© 1978, 1984 by International Bible Society

Scripture quotations marked NASB are from the
New American Standard Bible,
© 1977 by the Lockman Foundation

FOR INFORMATION.
MULTNOMAH PUBLISHERS, INC
POST OFFICE BOX 1720
SISTERS, OREGON 97759

99 00 01 02 — 10 9 8 7 6 5 4 3

CONTENTS

ANTICIPATION

REFLECTION

PREPARATION

CELEBRATION

EXPECTATION

INTRODUCTION

aze with me into the face of Joy!

Joy is more than merriment, more than happiness, and more than the other myriad of human expressions and experiences we use to describe happy fulfillment. Joy includes them all, but transcends them by leagues.

Joy is the inner knowing that everything you were ever meant to know and to be has been arranged for you—and is forthcoming, as you grow toward it.

Joy is the certainty that whatever leashes your life to less than Love, or whatever has stained your soul with shame or failure has been neutralized by the one power that can free and forgive us all—the living Christ.

He is the reason for Christmas. His name is on it, and so is the seal of His pleasure with all those who celebrate His coming.

I've arranged this small book to urge you to maximize the possibilities of such celebration. Here is a collection of thoughts, verses, and carols not only to point to Him who is the Way, but to provide a way for you to rejoice in His coming!

When angels sang, when prophets spoke, and when a star shone on high, they all said the same thing: Come and behold HIM. It is my deepest desire that the recollections, lyrics, and promptings contained in this little volume will echo that eternal word.

That's wisdom. Because any Christmas that brings you and me close to Him is one that not only brings us closer to a joy-filled season...it will bring us to the Fountain of Joy Himself.

His name is Jesus. Be blessed with the most joyous of Christmases as you allow me to share with you in re-joy-ing over His coming!

Jack W. Hayford
The Church on the Way
Van Nuys, California

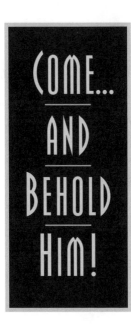

COME...
AND
BEHOLD
HIM!

ANTICIPATION

☆

Come, Thou long expected Jesus,
Born to set Thy people free;
From our fears and sins release us;
Let us find our rest in Thee.

I remember an evening this past year
when Anna and I stood with ninety people who
joined us in travel, and sang songs in the
shepherd fields near Bethlehem.

Amid the dark, twisted trunks of an olive grove,
under a night sky awash with starlight, we stood in the silence
and worshiped. A fresh sense of awe filled our hearts as we were
reminded . . . God sent angels to this site to tell men
He was sending Jesus to this place . . .
to save His lost sheep.

This Christmas, you come, too. Come . . .
stand in the shepherd fields with me. Come . . . kneel in the soft
radiance of a trillion stars. Come . . . and behold Him.

Wherever you are,
Jesus is as near as He was to the shepherds in Bethlehem on
that first Christmas night . . . and by His Spirit, even nearer
still. Wherever you are, you are standing on holy ground.
If you are reaching for Jesus, you needn't reach far.

He is here this Christmas to heal, to deliver,
to restore, to transform—to save you.

Hear that word and let us sing in these fields of
holiday celebration . . . together.

"WE'LL DRESS THE HOUSE..."

Splendor and majesty are before him;
strength and joy in his dwelling place.
1 CHRONICLES 16:27, NIV

nna and I drove to the mountains amid swirling leaves and a faint dusting of snow. Still basking in the glow of Thanksgiving-past, we let the weather tease us with a glimpse of Christmas-yet-to-come.

Never one to postpone the anticipation, I slipped a cassette of Alfred Burt carols in the tape deck, and together we enjoyed some of the finest music of the season.

We'll dress the house with holly bright and sprigs of mistletoe....

So begins one of Burt's many carols, mid-twentieth century masterpieces written year to year as the text of his family's Christmas cards. Some of his better known creations include "Some Children See Him," "Star Carol," and "Caroling, Caroling." These are songs which you hear once and feel you've known all your life.

But it was his "This Is Christmas," which begins with the phrase quoted above, that was most alive to me last week. Wherever I turned, "dressing this house" was exactly what was happening. At home, in my office, at the church, in our neighborhood—everywhere decorations are brightening homes and splashing workaday surroundings with the colors of the season.

In the midst of these transformations, it may be timely to reflect for a moment on this matter of "dressing the house" for Christmas. As a guide to your own decoration, I offer a few observations.

First: Be assured, this is righteous.

I mean it! Decoration of the house at Christmas is neither a surrender to pagan traditions nor a capitulation to commercialism.

Listen…

if God commissioned angels to roll back the night and fill it with blazing light,

if God provided a mighty celestial choir to serenade a few startled shepherds,

if God graced the heavens with a miracle star,

if God arranged such a memorable entry point as a feeding trough in a stable,

if God went to all this trouble to open our eyes to His entry into our world, then we needn't apologize for festooning our home with a few seasonal reminders!

Since the Light of the World has come, lights strung across the roof only "shout it from the housetop." Candles and candelabra, stars and starlight, gifts and giving, songs and sonnets,

lights and lightheartedness, angel cookies and wise-men ornaments—*all* are consistent with what transpired on our little
planet two thousand years ago.

"He will be great," Gabriel told Mary, "and will be called the
Son of the Highest" (Luke 1:32). The Great One was born
among us and born one of us! Is it any wonder that the echoes
of that great visitation roll down through the centuries and millennia? God lavishly spread wonders in our midst in the whole
flow of events surrounding the Advent of our Savior. That we
celebrate the memory with attention and care, the wonder-filled
and wonder-full, is entirely appropriate.

Second: Since it is right, sanctify it.

Present your decorating and decorations to the Lord as a tribute to Him.

Pray before you decorate.

Worship as you decorate.

Give thanks after you decorate.

As Paul writes it, "Whatever you do, do all in the name of
our Lord Jesus Christ giving thanks to God the Father by Him"
(Colossians 3:17).

A few days ago our entire church staff met in the sanctuary.
All the workers who were decorating joined together with us,
and we prayed and praised. We rejoiced with a carol, lifted up
spiritual song in worship, and then I prayed: "Jesus, we're

doing all this decor as a tribute to You. Please receive it—as an expression of our thanks for Your coming and our joy over Your life in us."

It was a tender time. And we enjoyed a fresh realization of Emmanuel—God *with* us.

Third: Invite others to share it with you.

When you "dress up," you usually "go out." But since our homes are fixed locations, the only alternative is to invite others in. It is a witness to our neighbors when they see a believer actually *happy* about life! So many in the world think us uptight and dour—incapable of genuine gladness. But when these neighbors and relatives encounter a home filled with true happiness, a light-hearted spirit of fun, and a warm, generous welcome, it can be utterly disarming. It paints a whole new portrait of the "Jesus life."

Remember, years ago, the country-western favorite which lilted the lyric: "You decorated my life"? Well, those are words we could well sing to Jesus Himself, for He has given us so much and brightened our world so grandly. And since He has, our decorations are simply another way of singing that song with godly gratitude.

It's going to be such a radiant celebration this year.

Let's dress our best.

(OME DWELL IN ME, JESUS

*"For my eyes have seen Your salvation,
which you have prepared before
the face of all peoples."*

LUKE 2:30-31

E ach year for over a quarter century, I've offered a pre-Christmas series of messages, inviting our flock at The Church On The Way to open hearts and homes to the miracle possibilities which Jesus' coming heralds to us all. Some of the tenderest moments of the year seem to be saved by the Holy Spirit for distribution in our midst during these weeks.

One year I brought a series entitled, "Coming Home for Christmas." Together, we studied the arrival of Jesus in the light of those who welcomed Him: the shepherds, Anna, Simeon, the wise men, each with a different order of readiness to acknowledge Him.

The shepherds were stunned by an angel-song and came in awestruck wonder (Luke 2:8-20).

Anna had waited on God for decades, lonely but unforsaken, and she announced Him as a long-awaited redeemer (Luke 2:36-38).

Simeon held a hope few would have granted him—

"Messiah shall arrive in my lifetime"—and he rejoiced in fulfilled promise (Luke 2:25-35).

The wise men left the security of home and country to seek the ultimate King. And they welcomed Him with their worship and unselfish gifts (Matthew 2:1-12).

One year as I was preparing for the first sermon of this series, I sat down at the piano in our living room on a Saturday afternoon. I remember feeling so very deeply the desire that every heart welcome what God was offering at the approach of Christmas. As I mused on these thoughts, the simplest, childlike melody began to fall from my lips, and I sang...with tears of expectant joy...

Come dwell in me, Jesus.
Stay, there's room for You.
Say what You will, Jesus.
Do all You want to do.

Perhaps you'll come and behold Him with that welcome, too. When asked, He always "comes in."

"Behold, I stand at the door and knock. If anyone hears My voice and opens the door, I will come in." (Revelation 3:20)

The Inescapable Christ

His life is the light that shines
through the darkness—
and the darkness can never extinguish it.

JOHN 1:5, TLB

I t was the day after Thanksgiving, and everything you might imagine the word "throngs" to represent surrounded us.

Anna and I were caught up and borne along by the crowds of Christmas shoppers on Fifth Avenue and then Madison Avenue in New York City. We had just finished brunch at Central Park's famous Tavern on the Green and had visited Saks to admire the decorations. We'd stopped to listen to a Salvation Army ensemble honor Jesus, then peeled and munched warm chestnuts bought from a street vendor, a delicacy which had literally been "roasting on an open fire." From there it was on to Bloomingdale's and Macy's.

It was in Bloomingdale's—one of America's most famous department stores—that it struck me again.

"Hark, the herald angels sing, glory to the newborn King," the P.A. system sang forth. We strolled past a display of wood carvings next to another one of fancy cosmetics.

"Jesus, Lord, at Thy birth," the closing words of "Silent

prospects His eternal covenant opens up to us. The promises of the Bible deliver meaning and hope to the highest of our desires and the deepest of our dilemmas. His every word is a solid reality upon which tomorrow's hopes can be placed and secured.

So let the visions dance in the eyes of your heart. Let faith see what your physical eyes cannot. Christmas dreams that root deep in God's own Word can never be disappointed.

"And you know in all your hearts and in all your souls that not one thing has failed of all the good things which the Lord your God spoke concerning you. All have come to pass for you; not one word of them has failed." (Joshua 23:14)

The Spirit of Christmas

So He came by
the Spirit into the temple . . .
LUKE 2:27

"Catch the spirit!"

"C'mon, get in the spirit of the season!"

These are common exhortations any of us might hear as Christmas draws near. At any season, the soul may linger in the shadow of circumstance, or lounge on a couch of cool reserve—either discouraged, distracted, or self-distanced from the bright possibilities awaiting us in God's ceaseless offers of goodness.

I was walking up and down the aisles of our church sanctuary one pre-Christmas day, praying for all who would come to worship the following weekend. No one else was in the room—except One. And that One, I knew, desired the well-being of the flock I serve—even more than I did.

He is the Holy Spirit.

As I walked from aisle to aisle, laying my hand on each empty chair and invoking His presence upon those who would sit there, a song began to spring up in my soul. It's a kind of "Mary song," who long ago was told by the angel, "The

27

power of the Highest will overshadow you...and God's promised purpose for you will be fulfilled."

Let the Holy Spirit of Christmas come upon you, too!

The Spirit of Christmas be on you this day,
The same Holy Spirit as there long ago.
Who filled Zacharias and caused him to say,
    "O blessed be the Lord,
    "Who is faithful to perform,
His promises of mercy He will now overflow."

The Spirit of Christmas be on you this day,
The same Holy Spirit who filled open hearts.
Elizabeth trusting was prompted to say,
    "You blessed who believe,
    "You surely shall receive,
Fulfilling of all things which God has said from the start."

The Spirit of Christmas draws near you today,
The same Holy Spirit fair Mary received.
He'll cause you to worship and teach you to praise,
    "O magnify the Lord,
    "For the power in His Word,
Brings mighty things to being, more than man can conceive."

The Spirit of Christmas would speak to your fears,
As angels to shepherds brought news of release.
And with that same message still speaks through the years,

> *"No longer fear, I say,*
> *For unto you this day,*

Is given you a Savior who shall fill you with peace."

The Spirit of Christmas be on you this day.
His presence fills with joy and His joy gives a song.
So open your heart to this carol and say,

> *"All glory be on high,*
> *And Jesus magnify,*

And Christmas joy will fill you now and all ages long."

THE LIGHT HAS COME

"His lamp shone upon my head,
...by His light I walked
through darkness."

JOB 29:3

I was flying home several Christmases ago and as my jet descended toward the Burbank airport, my heart leaped within me. The whole floor of the San Fernando Valley was a carpet of multi-colored lights woven from a million strands, composed of wire-like cords which string bulbs across rooftops. A hundred thousand window frames were embroidered in color, like ginger-breaded Swiss chalets.

My eyes teared up and I began to sing praises to God the Father...to Jesus the Son-given, and the Holy Spirit overflowed my mouth with worship. I was caught up in awe at the way God has, with majestic cleverness, "caught" mankind with Christmas. Inescapably, the glory creeps across the landscape worldwide.

None can deny it. *The Light has come.*

Man is trapped into testimony, and the lights declare it: *The Light has come.*

Suddenly, and for the most part unwittingly, across the face of the earth a billion of mankind rise with light in their hands to testify to it. It may not have even penetrated their hearts or their minds as yet, but with candles, torches, and bulbs they announce the fact: *The Light has come!*

I sat at my desk late the other evening, our family having just finished decorating our tree, and I wrote:

The Light has come and the darkness can
> *Never be the same, O hallelujah!*
The Light has shone and the darkness ran
> *Never to return, O hallelu!*
Your Word made flesh, Your Glory revealed;
> *Its entrance gave great light.*
You spoke, He came: Christ Jesus His name.
> *And He has scattered our night.*
The Light has come and the darkness can
> *Never be the same, O hallelujah!*
>> *And now the Light shines to ev'ry man.*
>> *You can live in light, O hallelu!*

The sound of joy fills the earth and sky and the bells
> *peal forth their hallelujah!*
The day has dawned and the sun climbs high,
> *for the Light has come, O hallelu!*
This Child now born, Himself is the Truth;

the Truth which sets men free.
His glory shines to all of mankind
and His light brings liberty.
The sound of joy fills the earth and sky and the bells
peal forth their hallelujah!
With freedom's song lift your voice and cry,
Jesus Christ is Lord, O hallelu!

A silver beam splits the sky above
and His star appears, O hallelujah!
A glory stream spreading hope and love
as Messiah comes, O hallelu!
He tramples darkness under His feet,
His battle flag unfurled;
Despair and bondage shatter and flee,
for He's the Light of the world.
A silver beam splits the sky above
and His star appears, O hallelujah!
His kingdom come is a rule of love,
casting out all fear, O hallelu!

The Light has come and for ev'ry man
Life has come to light, O hallelujah!
Tho' some resist it, they never can
overcome its power, O hallelu!

For God in flesh once walked on the earth
as Jesus, Son of Man.
The splendor of His glory displayed
continues ages to span.
The Light has come and to ev'ry man
Life has come to light, O hallelujah!
And as it shines unto me I can
Be renewed in life, O hallelu!

It's true. The undeniable reality which has ignited your heart and mine is flaming from housetops with an unquenchable message: "In Him was life, and the life was the light of men. And the light shines in the darkness…That was the true Light which gives light to every man who comes into the world" (John 1:4, 5, 9).

As this holy fire leaps higher this season, would you join me in a commitment?

Lord, I will not be satisfied with the wealth of joy and life You have caused to be mine, until I can share it with EVERY ONE. You have lighted the candle of my spirit; I will take it and touch others, until the world is purified by Your consuming flame.

A Quiet Corner of Anticipation

A crystal punchbowl sparkles in the candlelight…
Tree lights reflect a spectrum on the windowpane…
Visions of sugarplums dance in children's dreams…

Joy!

A spontaneous embrace is filled with
grateful affection…
The warmth of a relationship is renewed by a
simple greeting card…
Mom and Dad share a deep closeness as they watch
their children playing with new toys…

Joy!

Potpourri fills the house with the
scent of the season…
Cider tingles on the tongues of carolers just
finishing their rounds…
Loved ones, filled with lazy satisfaction following the
holiday dinner, surround the hearth…

Joy!

And most joyous of all…He is with us.

REFLECTION

How silently, how silently
The wondrous gift is giv'n!
So God imparts to human hearts
The blessings of His heav'n.
No ear may hear His coming,
But in this world of sin,
Where meek souls will receive
Him still
The dear Christ enters in.

The painting on the Christmas card
ignited every emotion that wintertime splendor can awaken.
The blue-white velvet of the snow, the web-like
silhouettes of the leaf-bare trees,
all surrounding a Tudor style cottage nestled center-scene.
The cottage windows glowing with light
reached straight from the canvas into my soul.
I could almost smell the cedar smoke rising from the chimney.

I reflected on that scene . . .
mindful again that the mood of this season is as
compelling a declaration of God's love as can ever be found.
Listen . . . He beckons to us . . .

Warmth . . . in a cold world.
There's a beauty to Christmas that is
sent with the snow, hangs crystalline as an icicle and
sweeps in like winter's crisp chill.

The sweetness of Jesus' name
is a savor which fills the heart and home of all of us
who have found Him.
"To you who believe, He is precious." (1 Peter 2:7)

Come home this Christmas . . .
And let the love of Jesus warm your soul.

UNWRAPPING CHRISTMAS

*And coming in that instant
she gave thanks to the Lord and spoke of Him to all
those who looked for redemption.*

LUKE 2:38

 hristmas month begins. And again I find myself wanting to reach out to help people who can't, by themselves, "unwrap" Christmas. It is, you know, "wrapped" for many:

…wrapped in the bandages of bygone hurts and disappointments

…wrapped in the plastic of sophistication which shuns childlike wonder

…wrapped in the tinsel of a materialistic binge

…wrapped in the confetti and streamers of empty partying

…wrapped in the busy-getting-ready preparations

…wrapped in the artistically designed whiskey box of bombed-out, so-called "celebrations."

The Ghost of Christmas Past returns to haunt numberless now-redeemed members of the Father's forever-family, but without the beneficial results produced by Scrooge's specter.

The "wrappings" represent the cluttered residue of a man or woman's private history. They are the wadded packagings of

Christmases ruined in other times, at other places. Sadly, the impact carries on, souring year after year. I'm speaking of people who

—had a heartbreak one Yuletide, and now always associate the season with that tearful memory

—have been burned out over family stresses surrounding the holidays, so that now these days are dreaded instead of anticipated with joy

—became wearied with the carnality of superficial gift giving when love seldom attended the presents, and now wince at the idea of Christmas shopping

How many cases? How many varieties of death wrap a God-appointed celebration of *life?*

I come to you today, my disappointed friend, in Jesus' name. And I come with this word: "Be free!"

Confront and reject those ghouls of past pain. Through Jesus—the Babe become King, the Son become Lord, the Child become Christ—in His mighty Name, lay hold of this festal day with rejoicings. Refuse to let the Prince of Darkness smother the Season of Light. The one who sought to murder the Baby of Bethlehem now seeks to ruin your celebration of His coming.

Resist him.

Resist him with all the strength your Lord provides.

Be untied. Be unfettered. Be unwrapped. Take my hands, and together...let's dance toward Christmas!

"Resist the devil and he will flee from you." (James 4:7)

"For you shall go out with joy,
And be led forth with peace;
The mountains and the hills
Shall break forth into singing before you,
And all the trees of the field shall clap their hands." (Isaiah 55:12)

CHRISTMASTIME WAS
MEANT TO BRING US LOVE

"My spirit has rejoiced in God my Savior."

LUKE 1:47

t was Christmas night, and the end-of-such-a-day anti-climax was starting to overtake us all. Afternoon dinner had been a festive highlight, following a morning filled with gifts, guests, greetings—and even more goodies.

The music of a Christmas TV special floated up the stairs to my study, where I'd been putting away a few gifts—and prodding myself to make a list for thank-you notes. I walked downstairs to an empty living room. Anna was in the kitchen, unloading the dishwasher, and the kids were scattered around the house in various stages of bedtime preparation—or sprawled on the floor with newly acquired games or books.

Suddenly my heart rose up in my throat—an emotion of such overwhelming joy I hardly knew how to express it. *"This is God's love!"* I breathed, with eyes misting and no one noticing.

I've felt it for decades. Christmastime—with all its loveliness, heart-warming habits, and traditions, and right down to the sweetness of candies and the fullness of tummies—was foreseen by the heavenly Father long ago. The sparse setting of a manger in a stable is worlds removed from the abundance of niceties which Christmas holds today. But it would be a mistake to scratch off the notion that God is in any way surprised at how "nice" Christmas has turned out to be. Listen, He *invented* it! And right along with "so great salvation" He has given us through His immeasurable Love and His unspeakable Gift, there are innumerable extras.

Enjoy them, too. They're all part of the love-gift plan. He designed Christmas to rejoice us in one grand eternal way, through giving us JESUS. But He is no less delighted to rejoice us in a multitude of temporal ways as well!

Christmas, tender and dear time;
Splendor, best-of-the-year time;
Precious, come-and-draw-near time;
> *For Christmastime was meant to bring us love.*

Christmas, go-buy-a-tree time;
Bright lights, let's-go-and-see time;
Laughter, wonderful-glee time;
> *For Christmastime was meant to bring us love.*
The gifts we give are but a small reflection
 of affection
 we feel.

The tenderness which fills our hearts is given
from heaven
to heal.

Listen, silver bells ringing;
Look up, angels are singing;
Reach out, Christmas is bringing to you
A priceless gift of peace sent from above.
   For Christmastime was meant to bring us love.

He is the Spirit of Christmas

"He Himself has said,
I will never leave you nor forsake you."

HEBREWS 13:5

 fire danced and crackled in the fireplace, our Advent candle flickered in the soft light, and the mellow voice of Nat King Cole wafted through the living room. We sat there...together.

Together as at all times of the year, yet together as at no other time of the year. Our family. Not all of us at that particular moment that one evening, but all together anyway. Maybe just Anna and me along with half our offspring, Jack and Christy. Mark? He's down the street baby-sitting at a neighbor's. Becki? She's married and well into Christmas traditions of her own.

But even with the scattering, we are together. Not just at Christmas...and yet, somehow, especially at Christmas.

Nostalgia, sentimentalism, seasonal emotion—none of the terms answer to this sense of fulfillment that fills me at this season. The finest quality of human love, the highest dimension of family devotion—neither adequately account for it. You can attempt to give an intellectual analysis of my psychological state or simply write off my condition as some adult stage of "visions of sugarplums."

But that won't do either. There is only one way to account for this.

Jesus lives at our house. And it's His birthday.

His presence is real, and the Holy Spirit communicates deep dimensions of His love among us. *He* is the Spirit of Christmas—*Holy* is His name. And whether you are thinking of the *Baby* in the manger, the *Child* whose parents escaped with Him into Egypt, the *Teenager* in the temple in Jerusalem, the *Prophet* scattering moneychangers' tables, the *Healer* restoring vision to blind eyes, the *Deliverer* liberating the demoniac, the *Teacher* revealing the truth of the eternal Father, the *Savior* dying upon Calvary, the *Lord* rising from the dead, or *Christ His Majesty* ruling on high at the Father's right hand...He's here this Christmas. The Holy Spirit makes that nearness very real.

You don't need candlelight and fireside glow to make it happen. Trees, ornaments, gifts, and all of it are splendid embellishments. Not necessary, but so very nice.

It's *Him*. He's finding more and more opened inns these days. It's priceless to discover the pleasure of His company, and especially when He's in a celebrating mood.

May your home know something of all this glory during these days. It's no Currier and Ives reproduction of something long ago. It's here. And it's now.

We've found the real thing.

Christmas Snow

Signs around are callin' homeward,
See the Christmas lights and snow.
Once again my heart is searchin'
> *For the child I used to know.*

Ev'rytime I touch this season
Deeper still it touches me.
As I watch this snow I'm thinkin'
> *Of the man I'm meant to be.*

Time and tides have often driven me
Some have charred and chilled my soul.
But I've heard I can forgiven be,
> *Whiter than this Christmas snow.*

Signs around are callin' homeward
See the Christmas lights and snow.
So this season I'm returnin'
> *To the place where I must go.*

There's a Hand that's reachin' to me,
There's a Love won't let me go.
There's a Voice that's callin' my name—
> *Callin' through this Christmas snow.*

Angels singin' in the heavens
Seems I see them in the snow
Shoutin' "Jesus has been given
> *To bring us to the Father's home."*

Singin',
> *"Christ the Lord is giv'n today, Hallelujah!"*
> *Hear the Christmas angels say, "Hallelujah!"*

I can hear the heav'nly Father
Say He wants me for His own;
He'll not reject or leave me
> *If this Christmas I'll come home.*

His the gift that keeps on givin'
Bethlehem was just the start.
His the love that keeps on livin'
> *Keepin' Christmas in my heart.*

Yes, I'm comin' home for Christmas
'Cause I have some place to go.
Father God, I'm comin' to You,
> *Thank you for this Christmas snow*
> > *Shinin' with a holy glow—*
> > > *Father God You love me so.*

Two Windows

"Sir, we wish to see Jesus."

JOHN 12:21

hroughout the ages, skilled artisans have sought to praise God through their crafts. Sculptors, painters, architects, and builders offered of their best for the glory of their Creator.

More than a few found this opportunity through the creation of magnificent church windows. In more recent years, stained glass has—sometimes and by some people—become associated with dead religious traditionalism. But this was not always so, for glasswork of this type was, for centuries, regarded as a high and worthy expression of worship and devotion.

Among those who cultivated this art form to its highest level was the renowned Louis Tiffany (1848-1933). While Mr. Tiffany's work as a creator of stained-glass lamps is more widely celebrated, his church windows constituted a far larger share of his creative efforts through the years. In fact, those world-famous Tiffany lamps were only an *afterthought;* only coming about because he needed to find a use for the left-over pieces cut from his window glass projects!

Not long ago, our congregation's Christmas decorations were dramatically enhanced by the addition of two magnificent Tiffany stained-glass windows, donated to our church family by long-time members. Originally created for a church in Pennsylvania in 1908, the windows were salvaged in the 1970s when the building was demolished. A few years later, the windows were brought out of storage at an antique auction, where they were purchased by our friends. They then sought the services of a uniquely gifted Pasadena artisan, who skillfully restored them, refitting the lead and replacing damaged panels.

The windows were lovingly hung in our sanctuary at Christmastime several years ago. When the workmen had finished and the windows were in place, I recall being stirred by a sense of wonder—not only because of their beauty and because of the Christmas timing, but mainly because of their *theme*.

The windows portray the Lord Jesus in His dual roles as Shepherd and King.

One window is a marvelous visual statement combining Psalm 23 and John 10; truth summarized by the great benediction of Hebrews 13:20-21:

"Now may the God of peace who brought up our Lord Jesus from the dead, that great Shepherd of the sheep, through the blood of the everlasting covenant, make you complete in every

good work to do His will, working in you what is well pleasing in His sight, through Jesus Christ, to whom be glory forever and ever. Amen."

The second window depicts Christ's ascension to a throne and eternal glory, as described in Acts 1:9-11:

"Now when He has spoken these things, while they watched, He was taken up, and a cloud received Him out of their sight. And while they looked steadfastly toward heaven as He went up, behold, two men stood by them in white apparel, who also said, 'Men of Galilee, why do you stand gazing up into heaven? This same Jesus, who was taken up from you into heaven, will so come in like manner as you saw Him go into heaven.'"

He came to be our Shepherd, laying down His very life for the sheep. He will come again as our glorious King, descending through the clouds just as He ascended before the astonished eyes of His disciples.

When the golden Southern California sunlight splashes through these twin windows, the portraits in glass catch fire, shining out in ageless blue, verdant green, snowy white, fiery crimson, and so many other hues from the glassmaker's rainbow.

At the time of their placement, I wrote: "This magnificence

in our midst is significant at this season, not only by its splendid addition to our Christmas decor, but because it prompts us to reflect on a deeper, more penetrating reality: Jesus came as the Great Shepherd of the sheep, guarding our souls and caring for us; but He is also King of our lives, reigning in power among us, worthy of profound worship and total obedience."

As we come and behold Him together this season, let's allow both truths to shine upon our hearts in all their color, wonder, and majesty.

"For there is born to you this day in the city of David a Savior, who is Christ the Lord." (Luke 2:11)

"You say rightly that I am a king. For this cause I was born, and for this cause I have come into the world." (John 18:37)

Come...let us adore Him!

That You Came is a Wonder

That You came is a wonder to me—
That You came in a manner so lowly,
Came to earth to live; came Your life to give.
That You came changed all history.

That You came brought the glorious Word—
Son of Man, named Jesus, the Savior.
What a Gift the Father gave,
His only Son He sent to save me.

That You came changed my destiny.
That You came is a wonder to me.

PEACE ON EARTH

*"The Lord lift up His countenance upon you,
And give you peace."*

NUMBERS 6:26

We were both cloaked in heavy coats and scarves as we strode along together, the skies above filled with winking stars etched into the inky backdrop of space. Christy, our youngest daughter, a junior high student at the time, was with me as we enjoyed one of our frequent walks—times we both look forward to. She was talking, her remarks initiated by the fact that a friend's house had recently been broken into and robbed.

"Ya know, Dad, it really makes me afra—well, not afraid, but it kinda bothers me when…ya know…all the stuff that's on the news…and like when bad things happen, like…well, robberies and killing and…you know, all that stuff…it sorta gets, well, it's so much like…I just wish like—that people would…ya know, Dad?"

Then, punctuated by a sudden waving of arms, her voice squeaked higher: "You know what I mean…I mean, like, I wish everything would be peaceful!"

I do know what she meant. It doesn't take the interpretive

skill usually necessary to understand an early teenager to feel what Christy was talking about. We all get tired of living in a weary world; a world worn by sin and death. A thousand manifestations of those two factors surround us, but the end analysis is always the same: The root is sin in the race and the fruit is death. Sin kills...it kills joy, hope, love, trust, peace, and, finally, people.

She continued. "Sometimes I think it would be so-o-o nice to live somewhere like Chippewa Falls [where her cousins live in Wisconsin]. Ya know, I mean, I like it here in Los Angeles, and all my friends, and our house, and my school, and...ya know, Dad."

"I know," I answered.

It was quiet a minute, our footsteps alone breaking the silence. I squeezed her hand reassuringly that I really did know how she felt.

"Chris," I began. "When you visited Amy and David in Chippewa Falls, were there any police cars there?"

She replied that there were, and I asked why she supposed so. She immediately got the point.

"I guess, Dad, because bad things happen everywhere... even in Wisconsin."

I went on, trying not to sound too preacherly. "Honey, there's no place in the world you can go to find peacefulness, because there's no place in the world to get away from people who hurt and who hate. Peace isn't something that's around you so much as it is something that is inside you."

We talked a lot more about that, and she evidenced that she really did understand. And was satisfied...truly. For peace is knowing (1) you are right with God, (2) you are right in your relationships, and (3) you are living where God wants you to be...in His will.

The angels' message, "Peace on earth," is not a tease or a taunt where open hearts will let peace work its wonder. And that peace will guard the heart that continues in confident surrender to the Father's will and way (Philippians 4:6-7).

ANGELS SANG AND SHEPHERDS HEARD

The shepherds returned,
glorifying and praising God.

LUKE 2:20

he same year I began my ministry as a young pastor, another young man my own age caught the spotlight of the nation. Elvis Presley's phenomenal rise to stardom—and equally tragic descent into personal failure and loss—is a matter of record now. Amazing numbers of people still mark and mourn his passing.

The first Christmas pageant we ever had was in our first, very small pastorate in Indiana. I wrote the program for our handful of Sunday school children to present. At that time, Presley had a hit song entitled, "Love Me Tender," which was written to an old Civil War tune with a haunting melody. I took that melody—which was on the lips and minds of almost everyone in America at that time—and wrote the lyrics below. It not only created a highlight for the evening, but it stated THE highlight of Christmas: We couldn't have been "loved more tenderly" than when God sent us Jesus!

Silence must have gripped the heavenlies in that hour, for the Son's exit was not on Christmas Eve. The song of angels would be withheld for thousands of earth hours yet to be. He wasn't leaving for a manger in Bethlehem, but for a *womb* in Nazareth.

God, a fetus. The most incredible concept of all.

How? What wonder is this?

Miracles and a resurrection are *easy* to believe once this truth is received: "The Word became flesh and dwelt among us" (John 1:14). Confidence in heaven's concern with earth's need is certain when we lay hold of the words, "Since we, God's children, are human beings—made of flesh and blood— He became flesh and blood too by being born in human form" (Hebrews 2:14, TLB).

God, a baby!

The ultimate vulnerability: God surrendering Himself to man. It extends beyond the limits of human imagination, but not beyond human comprehension. Because of the unimaginable I can experience the comprehensible. Because of the eternal expenditure that the Father made—giving His Beloved— and because of the redemptive price the Son would pay—giving His blood—I can be born again.

Forgiven.

Transformed.

Brought to the Father forever.

It is all finally comprehensible because it can happen in

me. But it somehow remains unimaginable when I attempt to conceive how His conception came about.

Yet it did.

And because of that morn, I awaken on this one to greet you.

From Heaven He Came

From heaven He came, O praise His name,
The Christ who took my shame.
King of all was He, yet He chose to be
But a man like me
So He came.

The Son of God, chose earth's cold sod
Left heaven's splendor rare.
And with naught to gain, Jesus stooped to claim
Man's despair.

He emptied Himself of all but love,
And came to a manger bed.
He stepped from heaven's home
To ascend a cross-throne; where a thorn-crown
Pierced His head.

So now acclaim this Jesus slain
Upon that cross for me;
All because He came we, by faith, may
Gain heaven too.

From heaven He came, to things mundane,
And stirred hope's dying flame.
Heaven's stars shone bright, angel choirs took flight
To proclaim the night
That He came.

On high He reigned, that vast domain
He left to take my place.
Heaven bended low that the earth might know
God's great grace.

Majestic robes were laid aside;
In swaddling clothes we see
God has come as a man
To complete heaven's plan and provide
Salvation free.

Behold this gift of grace and lift
Your heart in faith above.
Praise the Christ who came from that heav'n
To bring us God's love.

A DECISION IN DECEMBER

Those who sow in tears
Shall reap in joy.
PSALM 126:5

t is as clear as any memory in my life.

It was a Sunday afternoon in December. I stood at the bottom of the tall slide in the park. It wasn't the little six-footer, but "the HIGH slide the *big* kids play on." With all the persuasion my seven years of life could muster, I was assuring my three-year-old sister Luanne that it was okay to slide down.

"C'mon! I'll be here and *catch* you! It's okay!"

Suddenly, beyond the slide and across the sprawling park lawn, I saw my father coming—running toward us. His face was grim and his manner urgent. He wasn't frantic, but I knew something was wrong—terribly wrong. Something had shaken our little world. Luanne slid into his strong arms and gripping me by the hand, Daddy began explaining the news as we hastily strode homeward.

It was December 7, 1941.

Pearl Harbor had just been attacked by Japan.

Seven-year-olds don't think much about governments and

politics, but one thing is certain—they can feel the shock and pain of war. And even though it was a distant threat thousands of miles away, the impact of that moment was then and there engraved on my soul.

Half a century later, on another afternoon in December, those long-slumbering emotions reawakened as I listened to a speech by President George Bush on the car radio, as I was driving home alone from an appointment. The president's voice broke as he stood on the deck of the memorial ship in Pearl Harbor and paid heartfelt tribute to the heroism exhibited by so many on that unforgettable day. As I listened, a surge of emotion rose from some deep well within. My eyes filled with tears.

Before the tears could spill over, however, I pulled a chain on my emotions and *stifled* them. With some effort, I exacted a firm restraint on my feelings. I would *not* weep. I would be "mature." I would be self-controlled.

Glancing at the clock on the dashboard, I was swept by a stunning realization: even as that good man's speech reached my ears, it had been fifty years *to the hour* since a little boy named Jack Hayford had trembled with emotion over news about a faraway war he could scarcely comprehend.

That small boy had wept—not because he understood what was at stake, but because his daddy was upset…and because he, as a child, could allow tears without shame. Somehow, that child had understood that life could never be quite the same.

62

Yet fifty years later, driving up Balboa Boulevard on the very anniversary of those earlier tears freely shed, the older (and supposedly wiser) Jack Hayford was steeling himself against tears.

But why?

Why did I—*why does anyone*—wrestle to achieve this type of restraint? Aren't deep feelings worthwhile? Where is the shame in being moved by memories of the past or joys of the present? What gain is made by the "adult" exercise of pressing tears back into the soul?

I pulled up to yet another traffic light, still thinking about it.

The president finished his emotional salute to the soldiers and sailors of another generation: my daddy's generation. I thought of him again, the way he was on that December playground so long ago. I thought about Luanne, my little sister, now with the Lord, as is my father.

My emotions stirred again.

And I wept.

I *chose* to weep. I *chose* to allow my tears to flow. And listen, please, dear friend, it wasn't emotion that prevailed that winter afternoon, it was *reason*.

Before the Lord, I made a settled decision in my heart as I pulled into the driveway at home. From that moment on, I was *finished* with phony "adult male decorum." I decided that I was too mature a man to deny myself the wisdom and pleasure of allowing proper emotions their healthy release. To my view, this is wise at *every* season...but especially this one.

Love, joy, wonder, sympathy, concern, compassion—all the emotions of Christmas Past and Christmas Present—all the longings for Christmas Future—deserve to be *seen* if they seek to be. Life is too short to sacrifice precious moments by stifling their fullest expression of shared joy or pain.

Christmas emotions and memories—or any, for that matter—are too rare and valuable to quench in the name of "cool self-control" or adherence to some artificial "image."

My friends and family, my brothers and sisters in Christ, my neighbors and associates, all deserve to know my deepest feelings. I have *no reason* to shield people who know me from my real self, unless it be the lame reason of a tiresome pride over-wary of "emotionalism."

Healthy emotions, appropriately expressed, are not a surrender to an "ism" at all. Emotional*ism* is the quest of emotional experiences for their own sake. But that issue is far removed from plain, human *emotions*—simply allowing our feelings to add their God-given color to the spectrum of life.

It took fifty years to make that December decision, and I'm hanging on to it.

I will pursue maturity, yes, but a maturity that can disclose heartfelt feelings about life's most precious things.

Who knows? As time goes on, I just might become grown-up enough to really be a child at Christmas.

Make Me a Child Again

I'm alone this Christmas Eve beside this tree,
Yet a presence I can feel
Calls for me to honestly and humbly come,
And in His presence kneel;
To forsake the human pride that so controls me;
To come out from where I hide behind my fears;
To lay down the sophistry that prevents simplicity;
And with openhearted, childlike faith,
draw near…perhaps with tears.

Make me a child again, a child again;
Hear this Christmas prayer, dear God:
Give me a tender heart, a childlike trust;
Let my spirit be reborn.
I want a faith that knows your Father-heart,
To believe your words to me.
I want to understand, to take your hand,
To have children's eyes to see.

To be a child again, to touch a friend
With the love that You have shown.
To lay aside my fears, forget the years
I have tried life on my own.

I ask, O God above, just now remove
All my hardness, my masks, and sin;
And at this Christmastime, make me a child again.
And at this Christmastime, make me a child again.

Who is this Christ of Christmas?

*He has rescued us out of the darkness and gloom
of Satan's kingdom and brought us into
the kingdom of His dear Son.*

COLOSSIANS 1:13, TLB

ad enough holiday sweets for the moment? Want to sink your teeth into a real Christmas meal— perhaps a hearty steak dinner? The feast begins with a few simple queries:

Who is this Babe of Bethlehem?

Who is this One who became flesh?

Who is this Child who called forth songs of angels?

Who is this Christ of Christmas?

The answers to those searching questions have echoed and reechoed through the centuries since His humble birth on that first Christmas night long ago. Rarely has the answer come back with more ringing authority than from the pen of Paul to the church in a small town called Colosse, in 61 A.D.

Like a mighty bell, tolling clear and strong through the millennia, carried to every corner of the world by the wind of the Holy Spirit, Paul's declarations to the person of Christ leave no room for debate, no occasion for doubt.

Who is He?

HE IS THE REDEEMER— *"in whom we have redemption"* (1: 14).

We who believe on His name have been "qualified" (v. 12), "delivered" and "conveyed" (v. 13) into a new realm and kingdom, by means of a price once-paid to secure our freedom, our potential, and our fellowship.

Who is He?

HE IS THE REVEALER— *"the image of the invisible God"* (v. 15).

The veil of mystery is removed from the Almighty. No one need wonder what He is like—His Son Jesus has come to disclose His heart, His nature, His ways, His very being. Christ is the "image" of God, and reveals all of the Father we could ever want to understand (John 14:9).

Who is He?

HE IS THE CREATOR— *"by Him all things were created"* (v. 16).

That He is called "the firstborn over all creation" (v. 15) does not suggest the Son of God is a created being. Here's what that phrase means: Of all who have ever come *into* creation by means of birth, He is the first and only who was Himself the Creator. All things—in heaven and on earth—were made by Jesus the Christ and for His use, pleasure, and glory. He is both the means and the objective of all creation—the Source and the Supreme Goal (Hebrews 12:2).

Who is He?

HE IS THE SUSTAINER— *"by Him all things consist"* (v. 17).

Just as John 1:3 declares that He, the WORD, *spoke* all

things into existence, so this text affirms that it is the power of that creative word that sustains—literally, "holds together"—all things intact. Hebrews 1:3 tells us that He "upholds all things by the word of His power." Just as He creates (Hebrews 11:3), so He keeps.

Who is He?

HE IS THE LEADER— *"He is the head of the body, the church" (v. 18).*

Jesus not only is the Savior and Pioneer of the Church, He is its Lord and King. The text emphasizes that He has gained this position by reason of His proven power and authority demonstrated in His resurrection. He who created all beings and powers (v. 15) confined Himself within His own creation, and voluntarily submitted to death (Philippians 2:6-9). But to the dismay of hell, He rose from the dead, gave birth to the Church, and is now Lord over all.

Who is He?

HE IS THE FOUNTAIN—*"in Him all the fullness...dwells"(v. 19).*

His Lordship has been established to fulfill. His voice cries out in the busy intersections of the marketplace and in the quiet places of contemplation, saying, "I made you for Myself. I am Life overflowing. Come and find your fulfillment and satisfaction in Me." He is the Bread of Life, the Light of the World, and the source of life's Living Water (John 4:10, 14; 6:35; 8:12).

Who is He?

HE IS THE RECONCILER— *"by Him to reconcile all things" (v. 20).*

As the source of man's fulfillment, He is also able to deal with man's brokenness and despair. The Christ of Christmas embraces lives shattered by sin and stunted by dark circumstances. There is *nothing* He cannot repair, recover, or renew. The only limits are those established by our fears or doubts. Where either of those habitual liars seek to prevail, *answer them* with praise unto Him—who makes peace possible "through the blood of His cross."

He is all of these things...and infinitely more.

That's an enormous job description for any human, let alone a newborn baby.

Yet this is the very one Mary wrapped in swaddling clothes and cradled in her arms that holy night.

Come...let us adore Him!

THE TESTIMONY OF JOHN

The light shines in the darkness.

JOHN 1:5

atthew and Luke unfold the history of Christmas in tender stories that touch our emotions. But it is John who records the *heart* of Christmas, in towering statements that stretch our minds. In eighteen verses, the prologue to John's gospel unveils the most compelling, overwhelming concepts ever presented to mankind.

John 1:1-18

In the beginning was the Word, and the Word was with God, and the Word was God. He was in the beginning with God. All things were made through Him, and without Him nothing was made that was made. In Him was life, and the life was the light of men. And the light shines in the darkness, and the darkness did not comprehend it.

There was a man sent from God, whose name was John. This man came for a witness, to bear witness of the Light, that all through him might believe. He was not that Light, but was sent to bear witness of that Light. That was the true Light which gives light to every man coming into the world. He was in the world, and the world was made through Him, and the world did not know Him. He came to His own, and His own did not receive Him. But as many as received Him, to them He gave the right to become children of God, to those who believe in His name: who were born, not of blood, nor of the will of the flesh, nor of the will of man, but of God.

And the Word became flesh and dwelt among us, and we beheld His glory, the glory as of the only begotten of the Father, full of grace and truth. John bore witness of Him and cried out, saying, "This was He of whom I said, 'He who comes after me is preferred before me, for He was before me.'" And of His fullness we have all received, and grace for grace. For the law was given through Moses, but grace and truth came through Jesus Christ. No one has seen God at any time. The only begotten Son, who is in the bosom of the Father, He has declared Him.

THE WORD BECAME FLESH

He became flesh and blood
too by being born in human form.

HEBREWS 2:14, TLB

One Christmas past, my reading of the previous passage, John 1:1-18, stirred me to write the following carol. The melody was modeled after a brisk, ancient English seaman's chantey. As you take time with these side-by-side texts, stand in awe of the magnificence of John's declarations—the grandest truths ever given mankind. Perhaps—even as I phrased them to suit the pulse of my Christmas melody—you might find a new song rise in your heart as well.

The Word became flesh and has dwelt among us
And we beheld His glory.
The One begotten by God the Father
Now full of all grace and all truth.
Who from before all beginning was,
The Word begetting all that now is.
The Word became flesh and has come among us,
Christ Jesus, the Son of God.

The Word became flesh and the Light is shining.
The Light that enlightens all mankind.
The darkness has been unable to quench it:
The Light of the world now prevails.
As many as open their hearts to Him,
Become God's sons and He shines within.
The Word became flesh and has come among us
Christ Jesus, the Son of God.

The Word became flesh and the heart of heaven
Was opened to show us the Father.
No eye has beheld Him but in Christ Jesus
His grace and His truth are declared.
Still coming He enters all who receive,
His birth renewing all who believe
That the Word became flesh and has come among us
Christ Jesus—the Son of God.

A Quiet Corner of Reflection

A few thoughts to consider as you reflect on
Christmases Past and Present…

Time is my resource.

• "Lord, teach me to number my days
that I may apply my heart to wisdom." (Psalm 90:12)

• Prayerfully present your days to Him and
carefully account for your days before Him.

• A small tool can help here: a journal, a simple diary,
a marking of your calendar—something to keep
yourself apprised of the responsibility we all share for our
use of time, God's priceless gift.

I am able.

The astounding potential in each of us is God's promise.

• "The exceeding greatness of His power
toward us who believe, according to the working of
His mighty power." (Ephesians 1:18-20)

• "The acknowledgment of every good thing which is
in you in Jesus Christ." (Philemon 6)

• "I can do all things through
Christ who strengthens me." (Philippians 4:13)

Set in the context of God's gift of time,
only one thing awaits its release.

I must exercise my will.

- "Choose for yourselves this day whom
you will serve." (Joshua 24:15)

- "Be filled with the Spirit—today." (Ephesians 5:18,
the Greek tense is present— "Today!")

- "Your word I have hidden in my heart,
That I might not sin against You." (Psalm 119:11)

- "For sin shall not have dominion over you."
(Romans 6:14)

PREPARATION

Joy to the world! The Lord is come;
Let earth receive her King;
Let every heart prepare Him room,
And heav'n and nature sing.

"*Be it unto me . . .*"
It was the whisper
of a young woman's ready response to God
that opened to the miracle of saving grace
entering our world in the person of Jesus, our Lord.

"*To you, today, a Savior . . .*"
May your heart be equally opened to hear
and receive God's angel-promise to you
this Christmas.

MERRY CHRISTMAS (WITH CRAMPS)

As each one has received a gift,
minister it to one another.

1 PETER 4:10

I had a *deja-vu* of sorts a few Christmases ago. I had the opportunity to relive one of my earliest highlights of the season.

My first bicycle was the centerpiece of Christmas 1943.

World War II was in full swing, and with all metal resources committed to the material needs of the conflict, new bikes were impossible to come by. But somewhere, my dad had found and fixed up an old one, repainting it in the most stunning red-black combination any kid could want. It was a completely unexpected, now unforgettable moment when I was told, "Close your eyes! Don't peek!" and then was allowed to open them after the bicycle had been silently wheeled into the living room and placed by the tree.

My second bicycle-for-Christmas was in 1979.

I was equally unprepared for the surprise. But this time it was three weeks before Christmas—and there was good reason for the early delivery.

Anna and the kids had sat me down in the living room with the same stern admonition: "Close your eyes! Don't peek!"

Then I heard the patio door slide open. I knew something was coming in, and I couldn't wait. The kids whispered excitedly while the fire on the hearth chuckled with good cheer.

"Okay, honey," Anna said at last. "You can look now."

I looked. I laughed. I jumped in the air like a nine-year-old. The grin that took over my face lasted until my cheek muscles hurt. I hugged Anna and each of the kids. I was *really* excited.

The earlier-than-Christmas arrival of my new bike was timed to allow its availability for the Annual Hayford Father-Daughter-Bike-Outing. Christy, our youngest daughter, was eleven at the time, and our bike-riding junkets were becoming legendary. We rode together all the time, but my bike was old and fading fast. The new one made possible our pursuit of a Christmas dream. Each year, as soon as she was out of school, we set our hearts to really take a ride—to take a *long* one. As she grew older each year, the distances extended. We enjoyed being with each other, and we enjoyed the challenge of being stretched...together.

Now, with my new bike to match hers, we determined to go *fifty* miles. For neighborhood-type bikers, that's no small feat, and we braced for the event with high expectations.

It was a cool December morning when we set out, ready to make biking history in the San Fernando Valley! We pedaled down Hazeltine to Riverside Drive; east to Coldwater Canyon; south (but up hill, and I mean UP HILL) to Mulholland Drive;

west, with lots of ups and downs along the southern crest of our Valley's rim, past one beautiful overview after another. We went down Hayvenhurst, west on Ventura Boulevard, and wove a path ending up at the westernmost point—Fallbrook Avenue, in Canoga Park. Wending our way north and east we pedaled along the base of the dam near Rinaldi and Sepulveda, rode under two freeways (this IS Los Angeles)—glided down Laurel Canyon, and ended up home about six hours after we left.

The outing, however, was not without crisis. The year of my new bike—1979—will also be forever marked as the Christmas of "leg cramps to end all leg cramps!"

We had traversed about thirty-five miles of our course when I dismounted to wait for a stoplight where the holiday traffic backed up near Northridge's giant mall.

I'll never forget what happened when I tried to remount.

Agony!

Sharp, stabbing, gripping, and grinding screams of tissues suddenly lamenting abuse. "You haven't used us like this in twenty-five years!" my muscles seemed to be shouting. I dropped my bike and fell back on the grass at the edge of the curb—groaning and calling Christy to come back to rescue Dad.

She hurried to see what was wrong, looking so alarmed I had to quickly assure her it was only a set of cramps in my calves—not a heart attack! It took a few minutes, but with her help and a brief stint of walking in circles on the lawn near the mall, I regained pedaling capacity and we resumed without further incident. (I did walk with something of a mild limp as I strode to the pulpit the following Sunday...to the laughter of the congregation who knew the story already.)

I've often thought of that ambitious Christmas bike ride through the years. Riding those fifty miles with my daughter was a *stretching* experience. But the pain was good, and even the cramps had their place. (I'll always treasure the memory of my eleven-year-old praying so sweetly and fervently for her daddy.) And I also think there's a Christmas message contained in that recollection.

I've concluded that it's good to receive a gift that stretches you. It's good to experience a few cramps in muscles that would otherwise be sedentary.

It's good to be tuckered out rather than stressed out.

It's good to chalk up some adventure with loved ones, breaking old records, pushing out your boundaries, going where you've never gone before.

And with those thoughts in mind, I wish you a Merry Christmas...with cramps.

I wish you a Christmas that opens you to gifts of every kind—especially those our loving Father gives in Jesus. And I invite you to be stretched by the possibilities of His gifts.

Yes, really s-t-r-e-t-c-h-e-d.

Don't worry. You'll recover. I did.

Prayer for a Christmas Morning

Birth in me, I pray.
On this, Your natal day
A new fidelity
A new integrity
A deeper purity
That Jesus, you may see
the fullness of Your purpose
and Your way revealed in me.

As I'm kneeling here
With New Year drawing near
My hands extend to You
My heart is hungry, too,
For all that's old and new;
Of all You call me to—
that naught be lost,
whate'er the cost,
that You will find me true.

THE MAGIC OF CHRISTMAS

"Behold,
I will again do a marvelous work
Among this people,
A marvelous work and a wonder."

ISAIAH 29:14

n a period when satanic operations and methods are increasing and becoming more apparent, many of us, myself included, have withdrawn from the use of certain words.

The word "magic" is an example. Because of its relationship to superstition and deceptions, as well as to the realm of black arts and evil supernaturalism, one hesitates to use it. It seems its age of innocence is gone.

But C. S. Lewis redeemed the word "magic" for me in his book, *The Lion, the Witch, and the Wardrobe.* He qualifies and distinguishes the evil from the good by the use of the adjective "deeper." The land of Narnia may lie under a curse as a result of the White Witch's magic, but the "deeper magic," worked through the lion Aslan's death, breaks the curse.

Christmas is a "deeper magic."

Beyond the spell of lights, carols, gifts, goodies, ornaments, tinsel, holly, plum pudding, mistletoe, stars, and generally endless loveliness, it's the magic of one specific miracle that captivates me.

"The Word became flesh."

That's the magic—the deeper kind—of this majestic season. Unquestionably, the mightiest magic of all is reflected in those few words from the prologue to the Gospel of John. God entered the arena of man. But more than that…*He became one.*

God…a man.

Please note. That wasn't "Man…a god." That image was forever destroyed by the coming of the true and living God— as a man. That fact must be secured for any clear thinking to come to our race.

The slowness with which this truth is seen and accepted is precisely the pace of civilization's progress. And the degree to which it is disregarded, shunned, mocked, or attacked marks the exact degree to which an individual or nation digresses toward inevitable decay. Man not only *isn't* deity, but we are *helpless* until we acknowledge that He is the only God.

Every human system of redemption is based on the supposition that mankind can somehow recover its lost estate by the energy of the flesh. Carefully calculated programs of human genius ceaselessly attempt to reclimb the heights of our lost nobility and destiny. But all that the flesh can ultimately produce in its own strength is sweat. And the odor of the flesh's product is a commentary on its sufficiency.

No, flesh cannot become God. There is no magic that can work *that* miracle. But God did become flesh, and in so doing brought a "deeper magic" to our human possibilities.

Interesting, isn't it, how that one word "became" not only describes an entrance, but it also suggests a beautification. "The new coat you wore," we say, *"became you....* It was so *becoming."* God "became" flesh, not only in that He "wore it well" (and my, how Jesus did that!), but in that He also returned the possibility of "beauty" attending "flesh" again. Because Jesus became flesh, our very humanity has been eternally enhanced—enabled to glow again with glory in this life, and readied to be ultimately glorified in God's presence forever!

Think on that.

Let's let Christmastime breathe of its deepest magic into our hearts until it possesses our minds. It will alter and stimulate everything about our observance of the special season we now share. The Lord of Glory, as theology texts put it, "endless, eternal, and unchangeable in His being, filled with wisdom, power, and holiness," became human—yea, became a baby! And all to work the "deeper magic" of bringing to a race that had lost paradise a second chance to receive it again.

In that holy moment of God's incarnation, the pristine unseen world invaded the tainted tangible one, and the magic began. In His coming, the unreachable, untouchable God became reachable and touchable. And now, every broken man or woman who reaches to touch Him can be made whole.

That magic He worked in Galilee and Judea still works today in your town and mine. It comes where the divine word is spoken. This is no cheap "abracadabra" of myth, nor an incantation born of hell. It's the heavenly Word of "deeper magic" which not only entitles humankind to hope, but which names the person who brings it. For that "Word" which became flesh has a name: JESUS.

Say it with me.

Jesus!

Praise Him with me, as we come and behold Him.

He's not a magician, He's the Master.

He's not an illusionist, He is Reality.

Yet to say His name *IS* to discover the "deeper magic" we all need and seek. It's that which saves completely, restores entirely, and heals ultimately.

And it's all in the name.

Say it again.

Let Your Love and Joy So Glorious

Let Your love and joy so glorious
Settle o'er us,
Go before us,
As we join this Christmas chorus,
Heralding Jesus' birth.

Let Your light and let Your glory
Settle o'er me,
Go before me,
As I tell the Christmas story,
Jesus has come to earth.

Let Your Holy presence shower
O'er this hour,
By Your power,
Like a fragrant Christmas flower,
Spreading a holy mirth.

Jesus, life is what you brought us;
Came and sought us,
Truth You taught us.
Heaven's Gift, Your Blood has bought us,
Bringing us all new birth.

THE TESTIMONY OF THE TREE

*"I am living and strong! I look after you
and care for you. I am like an evergreen tree,
yielding my fruit to you throughout the year.
My mercies never fail."*

HOSEA 14:8, TLB

T he placement and decoration of a Christmas tree at our church as a part of our Christmas celebration is a specific statement, not an occasional or accidental surrender to cultural tradition. By means of this tree we are saying:

We believe in celebration.

We serve the God who "gives us richly all things to enjoy" (1 Timothy 6:17) and who through history assigned to His people sacred appointments of feasting and rejoicing. While God is neither a giddy Roman Bacchus nor a frumpy American Santa, He is the "blessed" and "happy" God (1 Timothy 1:11). Through Jesus Christ, He has introduced life "into the light." It is in this light that true celebration can be realized, rid of the carnal accessories of sensual practice and free of the ritualized accouterments of religious tradition.

We believe in sanctification.

God's grace not only provides for our personal progress in

purity and piety, but His Spirit flowing through our lives has a capacity to infuse our daily activities with righteousness. This means that amoral traditions may be seized upon by believers and converted to holy occasions and practices, so long as the Word and the way of the Lord are kept in primary focus.

We resist as an inert, deadly religious, and nonscriptural notion the idea that participation in such festivals as Christmas and Easter are heathen practices to be shunned by believers. Instead, we hold that *only* believers have access to the concepts which allow for the fullest and richest celebrations at such times. We do not flee the innocent cultural traits of celebration, but choose to instill them with deeper color by participating with enlightened understanding and pure living.

We believe in symbolism.

No one can verify the calendar date of Jesus' birth, but we accept December 25 as an annual day of declaration that "The Word became flesh," and that "Light has come unto the world." No one can validate the giving of gifts as a divinely appointed means of celebration, but since we serve a gift-giving God (James 1:17), we believe it appropriate to signal the occasion of His greatest gift as a time of sharing in the same spirit of love.

Although no one can make a "biblical case" for Christmas trees, we gather around ours with joy. We see in its living branches a symbol of everlasting life given us because of Jesus' death on *the tree,* at Calvary—whose naked crossbars Xed out death and ushered in forgiveness, regeneration, and eternal hope.

...The lights on our tree gleam a testimony of His Light-of-the-World glory.

...The ornaments reflect the decorative splendor with which His kindnesses adorn our personal and corporate lives.

...The star beams hope, with a heavenward ray, reminding us that it is from there He shall come again to receive us.

The season is upon us, and in celebrating it we make it His! For He has made all of life's loveliest things ours.

Winter Carol

When the fullness of time had come,
God sent forth His son.

GALATIANS 4:4

t was three days after Christmas. The spell of the season was yielding slowly to the approaching new year. Christmas morning's golden sunlight had been smothered by the leaden skies of a storm blowing into our southland setting.

The rain had passed for the moment, and though heavy skies still hung overhead, I wrapped myself in coat and muffler against the biting breezes and set out for a walk. I found a place of solitude on a nearby golf course—empty of players by reason of the recent rains—and enjoyed some quiet moments of worship as I strolled the path at the edge of the soggy fairway.

As I meditated on the stormy skies overhead and the bright, sunlit holiday just past, it struck me that Christmas had come at just the right time. Lingering on that thought for a moment, I experienced a sudden swell of emotion. How like the Lord! He sent His Son "at just the right time," as one translator renders Galatians 4:4. Not only did Christ appear at the very prophetic moment assigned by divine providence and not only did He come in time to answer the need of a fallen race, but He also foresaw the impact on *our* calendar.

Nothing can be more wearying than a long winter. Those who live in regions where ice, snow, blizzards, and penetrating winds reign for months on end know how depressing the season can be. Even for those in sunnier climates, short December days may bring bleakness of soul.

Noting a threatening cloud cluster on my own immediate horizon, I picked up my stride toward home. And as I walked, I hummed a new melody. At the same time, I found myself threading words around the tune—expressing gratitude for God's goodness in "breaking open our darkness."

At any season, He always comes on time, and this was the message—and the setting—that occasioned "Winter Carol." As you read it, do what it says:

"Let a carol rise! The Savior is here!"

Steel blue the sky and chill the night,
In which our Father gave the Light;
>   *Sent to warm our souls and*
>   *to drive away the cold.*
Let a carol rise, Noel, Noel, Noel;
Lift your voice, my soul, Noel, Noel.

Gray are the days of frosty clime,
Early the dusk at wintertime
> *When we sing anew how*
> *the Morningstar appeared.*
Let a carol rise, Noel, Noel, Noel;
Dark no longer feared, Noel, Noel.

Short tho' our days and soon our night,
Flick'ring our flame and dim our light;
> *Yet eternal life has been*
> *giv'n to man this Day.*
Let a carol rise, Noel, Noel, Noel;
Sing now and for aye, Noel, Noel.

Snowfall and starlight everywhere,
Glory surrounds this season rare;
> *For the Son of God now*
> *has come to us from heav'n.*
Let a carol rise, Noel, Noel, Noel;
Grace and peace are giv'n, Noel, Noel.

BECAUSE HE GAVE

Open your mouth for the speechless,
In the cause of all who are appointed to die.
Open your mouth...
And plead the cause of the poor and needy.

PROVERBS 31:8

I came across an article in a Christian journal several years ago, and I've never been able to escape the impact of its title:

FORGIVE US OUR CHRISTMASES,
AS WE FORGIVE THOSE WHO CHRISTMAS AGAINST US.

My first reaction was, "Why so dour? Why so negative a tone concerning such a happy season?" Then, almost immediately, I answered my own question. *Because there is so much done in the name of Christmas that is neither pleasing nor honoring to Christ.*

Even so, I find myself doing battle almost every year with those religious superstitions which argue against almost every observation of Christmas, calling it a pagan festival. Or against giving, as though it were a commitment to greed. Or against decorations, trees, or just plain fun, as though such participation defiled something holy. Such harsh debunking in the name of godliness is nothing more than "holy humbug." (And not all that holy, besides.)

Yet as much as I have resisted the cynical slams against Christmas festivities, I must be equally confrontive with a glib, silly, or shallow celebration of this precious day and season.

We cannot honor Him who was shunted to a stable by a world too busy with its commerce, if we overlook the little ones who are denied birth by a system that cares more for personal convenience than for human life itself.

And we dare not forget that the first Christmas was visited upon the lowly. The shepherds symbolize those who live outside the mainstream of society's life and commerce. They were little regarded, lightly valued, and possessed next to nothing.

If I would honor Christ with my Christmas giving, it must include doing something to help both these groups: the defenseless and the needy—the undesired infants and the overlooked poor.

If you would care to join me in this concern, here is my simple appeal: Would you take the equivalent amount you are spending for one of your nicer gifts this Christmas and make a gift—in Jesus' name, in Jesus' love, and in remembrance of the Bethlehem Babe they tried to kill?

I'm thinking of the Crisis Pregnancy Center nearest to you.

I'm thinking of those advocacy groups that speak out boldly and tirelessly in the name of Jesus for the rights of the pre-born.

I'm thinking of one of the fine Christian groups that sponsor poor children in Third World nations.

I'm thinking of your church's ministry to the distressed and disadvantaged in your own community.

Let's glorify Jesus this special way, remembering His entry into our world as a humble, helpless baby.

It's another way to sanctify the season—and keep it as *His*.

Night Like No Other

On this night like no other a young virgin mother
Bent low with the pain of new birth.
While beside her in wonder a strong, loving husband
Awaited God's gift to the earth.
Humankind seemed unable to sense that a stable
Could harbor the birth of a King.
So the heavens before us broke forth in a chorus
To sing and to say
That in that manger lay
God in flesh now appearing, Salvation is nearing
The earth-hope for peace now has come.
Open hearts now receive Him
Fear not to believe Him,
The Savior of man,
Here fulfilling God's plan
In the Person of Jesus has come.

* * *

On this night without equal our God wrote a sequel
To man's hopeless legend of loss.
What began in a garden cried out for a pardon,
God soon would provide through a Cross.
For that dear baby's crying now forecasts a dying,
His coming is planned to bring life.
And this heaven-sent stranger now laid in a manger,
Is God come to heal
And God's love to reveal
God in flesh now appearing, Salvation is nearing
The earth-hope for peace now has come.
Open hearts now receive Him
Fear not to believe Him,
The Savior of man,
Here fulfilling God's plan
In the Person of Jesus has come.

LIVING ABOVE CONDEMNATION

*For God did not send His Son into the world
to condemn the world, but that the world
through Him might be saved.*

JOHN 3:17

here is the "merry" in "Merry Christmas"?
Where is the "joy" in "Joy to the World"?
Where is the "happy" in "Happy Holidays"?

Answer: The soaring gladness of Christmas is directly linked to God's gift of Jesus to us and for us.

The Son of God has come,
Light has entered the world,
a Savior is here and
our sins can be forgiven!

Apart from these glorious facts, there is no logic to the season's existence, much less for festive rejoicing. The day before us derives its meaning and highest fulfillment from this radiant reality: *God is with us!*

We rejoice because Joy has come to earth.

We give gifts because the Best and Grandest has been given to us.

We feast because the Bread of Life has been provided.

We sing carols of endless variety because all of life has been penetrated by The Song.

Still, amid all the brightness, innumerable souls remain shadowed. The power of human failure to stain the soul is immeasurable! Years afterward, darkness shades tomorrow's horizons. The impress of guilt leaves ridges in the mind, and in the valleys beneath them shafts of sunlight rarely appear. Condemnation is a dark demon which shrouds the soul, stifles hope, and suffocates confidence for tomorrow.

The lighting of our Christmas candles is a picture of an uncontainable joy that burns out these shadows of half-life and living death. This Christmas Eve we praise the One

...who came to break the back of condemnation

...who came to restore us to union with our Father Creator

...who came to cleanse and purify our souls through His cross

...who came to fill us with God's Holy Spirit

...who came to enable us to become all we were meant to become.

John's gospel records Jesus' words which explain the one reason condemnation remains in any heart: "This is the condemnation; that light has come into the world and men love darkness rather than light, because their deeds were evil" (3:19). In short, the only people who need bear condemnation from God are people who prefer their own way to His.

So, as you take your Christmas candle in hand, join me in a dual declaration:

• I receive Your light, Lord Jesus—purge my soul and let me live in the warmth Your light gives.

• I will share Your light, Lord Jesus—that having so freely received of Your love, I will spread the love-brightness You've ignited in me.

Sing it again...

The Light has come and the darkness can never be the same...O Hallelujah!

Joyful, Joyful, Christmas Morning

(SING TO BEETHOVEN'S "ODE TO JOY")

Joyful, joyful, Christmas morning,
*   Hail the Savior come to earth.*
Worshipping we come before Thee,
*   Praisefully extol Your worth.*
As the angels long before us,
*   Sang the wonder of this day,*
We exclaim the joyous chorus,
*   "Grace and peace have come to stay!"*

Joyful, joyful, we adore Thee,
    Child foretold by prophets' voice.
Virgin-born in Bethlehem.
    A Son is given, now rejoice!
Wonderful and Counselor
    And Mighty God be called His Name;
Everlasting God among us,
    Prince of Peace now come to reign.

Joyful, joyful, we adore Thee,
    Lamb of Bethl'em's manger stall.
We have heard the heav'nly message,
    "Born a Savior for us all."
Like the shepherds coming to Thee,
    We have found the King of Life.
Manger Lamb once slain to save us,
    Risen Lord and Reigning Christ.

Joyful, joyful, we adore Thee,
    Babe announced by radiant star.
Beckoned by God's glory-shining,
    Wise we come to kneel this hour;
Spread our treasures, here before You,
    Heart in hands raised up to Thee.
Take my gold and myrrh, O Jesus;

All I have and all of me.
Joyful, joyful, we adore Thee,
King of Kings and Lord of Lords.
On this Christmas Day we offer
All the praise our hearts afford.
Holy Spirit overflow us,
Free our tongues to help us praise.
Give new gifts for praising Jesus,
Laud we Him this Day of Days.

A Quiet Corner of Preparation

• Build into your schedule some just plain enjoyable time.

• Keep a jigsaw puzzle going.

• Have some hot cider mix near at hand, to add to a few
minutes of relaxation in the midst of preparations.

• Read stories to your children, or even take time
to nap with them. If you want them to be peaceful,
be peaceful with them!

• Moms, don't forget how much children love to help
with cookie making. (Sampling is really their forte.)

• Be sure you include times of talking, reading, or
discussing with your family the real meaning of Christmas.
(No matter how old they are!) A time of concentrating on that
Most Wonderful Gift will set an atmosphere
in your home that cannot come any other way.

• Use dinner time this month to read the Christmas story—
in installments or from a Christmas devotional.

• If you're unmarried, a single parent, or even a
young couple far from your families, start traditions
of your own. Invite other singles to share your
celebration of Christ's birth.

• If all the preparing and running around become too much,
follow Mary of Bethany's example and sit for awhile at
Jesus' feet. (She had her reward…and so will you!)

CELEBRATION

☆

Joy to the earth! the Savior reigns;
Let men their songs employ;
While fields and floods, rocks,
hills and plains
Repeat the sounding joy.

May the glory of
His goodness fill your heart and your days
With the Light of lights . . .
The Morningstar . . .
The Dayspring from on high.

And in that light,
May the gentleness of His grace overflow your soul,
And high praises attend your celebration
of Jesus' birth.

The Lost Art of Celebrating

So they ate and drank before the Lord
with great gladness on that day.
1 CHRONICLES 29:22

verything about Christmas brings excitement and joy.
But in much of our society, celebrating is a lost art.

In today's world, celebration generally involves one of two things: getting stoned out of your mind on booze or drugs, or spending more than you can afford. It may involve anything from a wild party that ends up in an orgy, to jumping on a plane and heading for Tahiti. Because of the pollution of celebration, many believers hesitate to celebrate at all. Can such a thing really be godly?

In the Church, as well as the world, we need to recover the lost art of true celebrating. Our situation is not without precedent. In the book of Nehemiah we find another case where God's people needed instruction in celebration.

Nehemiah 8:8-12 describes a scene in the open square in front of one of the great gates of Jerusalem, where the people had gathered to hear the reading of the Law. Ezra, the scribe, stood on a platform and read, while others of the scribes and

Levites scattered through the great throng to help the people understand what they were hearing.

> "And Nehemiah, who was the governor, Ezra the priest and scribe, and the Levites who taught the people said to all the people, 'This day is holy to the LORD your God; do not mourn or weep.' (For all the people wept, when they heard the words of the Law.)
>
> Then he said to them, 'Go your way, eat the fat, drink the sweet, and send portions to those for whom nothing is prepared; for this day is holy to our LORD. Do not sorrow, for the joy of the Lord is your strength.'...And all the people went their way to eat and drink, to send portions and rejoice greatly, because they understood the words that were declared to them." (Nehemiah 8:9-10, 12)

Emerging from a long and demoralizing captivity in a foreign land, many of these people were hearing the Law of God for the first time. As they became aware of their own inadequacies— their appalling failure to measure up to the standards of this God of their fathers—sincere tears began to flow, and they grieved.

But not for long!

Nehemiah and Ezra instructed the other leaders to stop the people's crying. They said, "Wait! Stop! You don't understand! There is a right and proper response of repentance, but this day is holy to the Lord your God. Lift up your heads. Wash your faces. Dry your tears. Don't mourn or weep!"

Many people don't realize that the original derivation of our word "holiday" is from "holy day." So when Nehemiah and Ezra said, "This day is holy to the Lord," what they were saying was, "This is a holiday! It's time to celebrate, not to be down-hearted and sad."

And they gave the people instructions on *how* to celebrate.

When they said "eat the fat" they were talking about eating meat. But I like that it says "fat." It was like saying, "Go ahead and enjoy yourselves! Eat what you like." Today we might say, "Go for it! Have two desserts!"

When the leaders said, "Send portions to those for whom nothing is prepared," they were talking about giving presents to each other—delicacies and food baskets and bounty from their tables.

"So they went their way to eat and drink and send portions and rejoiced greatly because they understood..."

Why didn't they understand before? Because they had lived in captivity too long. They were too well acquainted with exile, estrangement, and loss. Now they were free and back in the circle of life in the living God and they didn't know how to live in His ways. They didn't know how to celebrate in the light of God's wondrous, liberating Word. Still feeling the weight of non-existent chains, they couldn't lift their arms in worship. Still feeling the oppression of captors left far behind, they couldn't throw back their heads and laugh.

They had to discover for themselves that they were really free.

They had to discover for themselves that the joy of the Lord was their *strength*.

And so I believe, must we.

Give Me A Voice, Lord

Give me a voice, Lord, to herald Your birth.
Give me a song, Lord, to sing of Your worth.
Give me a tongue, Lord, to shout out Your praise,
And I'll sing Hallelujah till the end of my days!

CHORUS:
Hallelujah! Hallelujah!
Sing the angel song, Hallelujah!
Peace on earth, and goodwill to men.
Worship Christ the King—Hallelujah!

Jesus is coming, He's coming to earth.
Jesus the Savior, the Lord of new birth.
Jesus my master, we're singing Your praise,
And we'll shout Hallelujah 'til that Day of all days.

JOY: THE CALL AND THE CONVICTION

*"So the ransomed of the Lord shall return,
And come to Zion with singing, With everlasting joy on their
heads. They shall obtain joy and gladness;
Sorrow and sighing shall flee away."*

ISAIAH 51:11

e who believe—"the ransomed of the Lord"—have been described as "the happiest people on earth!" Contrary to some people's assessments, such happiness is neither superficial nor glib.

It is more than excitement.

It excels enthusiasm.

It transcends emotions.

It soars above "positive thinking."

It is not dependent upon circumstances.

Its genuineness is due to its source, for the wellspring of happiness is a fountain named JOY. Unlike earthly notions of "joy" (used interchangeably to describe everything from a surge of hormones to a trendy perfume), the genuine article is an eternal, definable *something*.

Joy is a God-given emotion…an internally sounding chord which resonates to the deepest wooings of the Almighty. It begins as a call and becomes a settled conviction.

The Call

Joy begins when you and I, creatures of the Creator, recognize and delight in His personal handiwork around us. We experience this

—in an autumn sense of longing

—in an infinity of starlight

—in an ocean wave of grandeur

—in a whisper of wind through summer leaves

Something within tells us these feelings are more than "aesthetic." They are beacons of eternity, summoning our souls to harbor in the security of the Creator's purpose. As David wrote:

"The heavens declare the glory of God;
And the firmament shows His handiwork.
Day unto day utters speech,
And night unto night reveals knowledge.

(Psalm 19:1-3)

Wise men respond to these longings by seeking Him, the Creator. And when they do, He promises, "you will seek Me and find Me, when you search for Me with all your heart" (Jeremiah 29:13). That discovery, of course, comes through encounter with Jesus Christ, in whom the fullness of the Creator's purpose and redemption is centered (Colossians 1:16-19). And from that point, joy increases!

The Conviction

Joy builds as the believer awakens to the assurance that the Creator who made him and redeemed him is committed to keep and fulfill him. As that conviction begins to overflow the soul, joy abounds. God's highest purpose and destiny has become guaranteed to us! (1 Peter 1:8). We have become impossible-to-lose, destined-to-triumph people (Romans 8:37-39).

Whatever trial, tragedy, stress, or disappointment I may face, joy remains constant. It continues to rise from the wellspring of God's loving purpose for me—I am *of* Him, He is *with* me, and—no matter what, I will *win*. Once that deep-seated confidence possesses you, and the conviction of certain triumph grips your soul, you come to understand the meaning of the eternal word: "the joy of the Lord is your strength" (Nehemiah 8:10).

Yes, we are happy people. But this is not a "happiness" that skips like a flat rock across the surface of pleasant situations. This is not a "happiness" tied like a kite-tail to feelings that change with the wind. This true happiness derives from joy— an artesian fountain that cannot be stopped by man or demon. God's Holy Spirit pours it forth, so let us live in its fullness.

And again I say, *rejoice!*

Send Your Glory, Lord

May the glory of God be upon us
    this Christmastime;
May the Spirit of joy be outpoured,
    That the blessing intended to be sent from heaven
        Now abound as we worship the Lord.

May the Bethlehem Babe be born in us
    this Christmastime;
May the blest tender grace of this Child
    Be incarnate again, be revealed in our living,
        As we walk in that Light undefiled.

As the shepherds we come from our task
    Lord, this Christmastime,
To respond to the message from heav'n;
    For Our souls pulse anew with this bright expectation
        That a Savior this day has been giv'n.

Father God, now we humble our hearts
    at this Christmastime;
To request that Your wisdom divine
    Lead us past all diversion until, as the wise men,
        We rejoice in Your Morningstar's shine.

May the glory of God be upon us
  this Christmastime;
May the Spirit of truth free us all.
    Broken yokes loose our lives unto Your celebration
      As Your love-gift our hearts now enthrall.

CHORUS:
Send Your glory, Lord
    (Send Your glory, Lord)
This Christmastime
    (this Christmastime)
Jesus, be adored
    (Jesus, be adored)
This Christmastime
    (this Christmastime)
That the glory,
    the glory of the Lord
      be revealed in this place.

"HOUSE OF BREAD"

*He said, "I am the bread which
came down from heaven."*

JOHN 6:41

orever honored as the town where our Savior was
born, Bethlehem was so named because it was a
center of wheat and meal production—crucially
important to nourishing and sustaining the people
of ancient Israel. How poetic and prophetic that God's Son—
the Bread of Life—would enter this world at a site named
"House of Bread"!

Your family treeside time can be the loveliest ever this year
as you open the Written Bread (God's Word) and read together
of the Living Bread (Jesus the Lord).

Invite each family member or guest to have a small part.
Some evening drawing near Christmas, gather at your tree and
let the sharing of the *whole* story unfold among you. If each
one takes a selection (after briefly becoming familiar with that
small portion of God's Word) the effect will be moving and
memorable. All will be reminded of the gift which is at the
heart of Christmas.

A simple reading outline may help:

Retelling the Story

1.

The announcement to Mary:
"You will be Messiah's mother." *Luke 1:26-38*
The announcement to Joseph: "This Child is God's Son."
Matthew 1:18-25

2.

The trip to Bethlehem:
"No room in the inn." *Luke 2:1-7*
The announcement to the shepherds:
"Go to Bethlehem and see!" *Luke 2:8-20*

3.

The visit of the wise men from the East: *Matthew 2:1-11*
The warning of Herod's threat
and the flight to Egypt: *Matthew 2:12-15*

4.

The prophecies God gave to us *about* Jesus:
Isaiah 7:14; 9:6-7; 53:2-6
The promises God has given to us in Jesus:
John 3:16-17; 10:9-11; 17:3; 20:31

After you've read the timeless story, you might also allow a brief time of prayer—inviting the Holy Spirit to reveal Jesus again. He's the King of Christmas!

To make the time even more memorable, I suggest what may become a new tradition for your family. Take a small loaf of fresh-baked bread, break it, and eat it together, quietly remembering the one born in the "House of Bread"...the one who was broken so that we might be whole...the one who offered Himself as the very Bread of Life.

Jesus, Come Again This Christmas

Jesus, come again this Christmas
Come O Lord Emmanuel;
Jesus, come again this Christmas
To this house to dwell.

You who came to Bethlehem,
Became a baby born to die;
Come again to reveal Your pow'r
As the King of Kings on high.

Jesus, come again this Christmas
Come, O Lord Emmanuel;
Jesus, come again this Christmas
To our hearts to dwell.

GOD'S GREAT GIVEAWAY PROGRAM

*Thanks be to God
for His indescribable gift!*

1 CORINTHIANS 9:15

 s we enjoy this season of gift-giving, I'm reminded of something unique to our American culture. I refer to our bombastic, super-galaxy-of-gifts, television giveaway programs.

As commercial and Madison-Avenue-packaged as they are, I must confess that in at least a couple of respects this cultural trait mirrors something of God's methods.

I see two parallels: (1) The recipient receives something free, and (2) the giver distributes from the abundance of his resources.

Theologically, we would call the first "grace" and the second "omnipotence." What God gives us is completely unearned, and the way He gives is from the abounding provision of the Almighty, All-Sufficient One.

From the moment of my entry into the saving life Jesus has given me through the cross, all the way through my lifetime of learning to walk in His love and power…it's all grace. He *gives* it. Nothing is earned. Nothing is accomplished through my strength or power. As the hymnwriter put it, "He giveth, and giveth, and giveth again."

And, of course, the second feature of this tandem-truth is the resource from which He gives. It's boundless, measureless, unlimited, unending, abundant, almighty, and eternal.

Be comforted and emboldened in your faith, this Christmas season. With every gift you purchase and every gift you wrap and every gift you place under the tree, remember this: *God has gifts for you, and in quantities you never dreamed.* These gifts are infinitely more valuable than the tinsel and materialistic toys pursued so desperately by the world. He has gifts of peace, strength, joy, fulfillment, and a sense of significance in life that will draw you out of bed each morning like a magnet.

He's looking for people who will come in simple dependence upon His grace and rest in simple faith upon His greatness.

At this very moment, He's looking your way.

Look up and see.

And open your hands.

I Take This Light

The people who walked in darkness
have seen a great light.

ISAIAH 9:2

 hristmas Eve is always marked by throngs hurrying homeward or away to visit relatives. Yet in spite of the bustle and hurry, an enormous host stops each year at The Church On The Way for our annual candlelight service.

For many of us, it is an hour that sets the rest of our celebrations in focus, sanctifying the day. A tender and touching "sharing of the Light" occurs as candlelight passes throughout the room. Every year, many make personal decisions for Christ as the flame is passed and the gathered worshippers sing the simple carol below.

I take this light on this Christmas night,
And I give of His light so true.
In Jesus' Name, now receive the flame
Of the love heaven sent to you.

For the Light has come and the Truth has shone
In the face of Christ the Lord,
So, this Christmas Eve, come now and believe
And receive the Light of the world.

IT'S MORE THAN MERELY "MERRY"

Building yourselves up on your most holy faith,
praying in the Holy Spirit.

JUDE 20

ou might expect the pastor of a large flock to receive lots of mail at this time of year. What you might not expect is the sheer amazement contained within (and between) some of those handwritten lines.

Often, they are letters from those newly associated with our fellowship who have allowed themselves—perhaps for the first time—to enter into the wonder and fullness of Christmas joy and celebration.

"I have never realized what Christmas could mean in terms of a truly happy time."

"My upbringing had been one in which Christmas was attacked rather than celebrated, but now…"

"I can hardly describe what Christmastime at our church did in my spiritual life—through ENJOYMENT of all things."

All in all, Christmas becomes more than merely "merry."

Christmas is *mighty*.

It was always intended to be.

Celebration—unfettered enjoyment, love and laughter, gifts and giving, trees and tinsel, holly and reindeer, carols and bells, pageantry and celestial music—*all of it*—I mean A-L-L of it—has an inherent potential for mightiness.

The qualifying factor is *the presence of the Holy Spirit.* When He is present, all the accouterments of Christmas have a tender power which can bless, strengthen, heal, restore, and bring entry into God's broad blessings of salvation.

When He is absent, carols ring hollow. Greetings, wishes, and smiles lie on the surface, like glitter glued on a flat card. Lights and decorations are only so much window dressing, which can leave the heart more desolate than ever.

But where the Holy Spirit is, there is *power*.

—Power to change entrenched attitudes.

—Power to transform cold hearts.

—Power to overthrow old habits, grudges, and expectations.

—Power to lift lives out of the shadow.

As Isaiah prophesied,

"The people who walked in darkness
Have seen a great light." (Isaiah 9:2)

Paul describes very clearly what the Holy Spirit is able to do in a life, in a home, in a church that yields to Him.

"For the weapons of our warfare are not carnal but mighty in God for pulling down strongholds, casting down arguments and every high thing that exalts itself against the knowledge of God, bringing every thought into captivity to the obedience of Christ." (2 Corinthians 10:4-6)

This Christmas, let Him come upon you.

Welcome the Mighty One, the Holy Spirit of Christmas, to move upon your life, and then…make your *own* move. Move into real celebration. Move into the season's best opportunities to worship and sing and bask in the wonder of it all. Move into your own family circle and neighborhood. In the power of the Spirit, reach out to those around: encourage, bless, bake, give, visit, invite, share, and lift hearts wherever you can.

By the time you reach the New Year, I promise you'll have found Christmas to be more than merely merry. It will have proven to have been marvelously, and even possibly miraculously, *mighty*.

Look to the Brightness

Look to the brightness, hark to the bells,
> *Hear now the carols, joy and gladness swell for*
> > *Christmas, Christmas,*
> > > *Merry, merry Christmas is here.*

Light has been given, look to the Child.
> *Love sent from heaven, shining undefiled for*
> > *Christmas, Christmas,*
> > > *Holy, holy Christmas is here.*

Look to the brightness, deck now the halls
Hear now the laughter, all our hearts enthrall for
Christmas, Christmas;
Happy, happy Christmas is here.

Open your arms, embrace every friend
All be forgiving, unforgiveness end for
Christmas, Christmas,
God's own gift of Christmas has come.

God's joy and peace give, In His release live,
Light every home, every heart with His love.

Joyous traditions fill holidays,
Our one condition; join them all to praise
The Lord of Christmas,
Make a merry Christmas His way.

Look to the brightness, see now the Babe
Bow low in wonder, glory here displayed for
Jesus, Jesus—
Son of God to greet us is here.

Soft now our voices, tender the word—
This tiny baby is the Lord of lords, praise
Jesus, Jesus—
Newborn Prince of peace—He is here.

Darkness will scatter, starts now the dawn
  Bondage is breaking, from this moment on
    God's Kingdom power
      like the sun increases each hour.

  Noel, noel, noel, noel
  Sing now noel let the bright carols tell.

Look to the brightness, hark to the bells,
  Hear now the carols, joy and gladness swell for
    Christmas, Christmas,
      Merry, merry Christmas is here.

YOUR PRE-CHRISTMAS TREE

"Nevertheless I have this against you,
that you have left your first love."

REVELATION 2:4

Years ago, I wrote a carol calling one and all to *"gather 'round the tree and dance with me, for Christmas time is here—that lovely time of yearly joying!"*

Without diminishing my commitment to such out-right expressions of gladness during this time of year, I believe God's Spirit calls us to a dual focus in the days prior to Christmas.

He calls us to the *holy* as well as the *happy.*

In some of my own time in the Word in recent days, I've pondered the story of Jacob's long, round-about return to Bethel as a rather unorthodox "Christmas story" (complete with angels, gifts, and a tree, Genesis 32-35).

"Then God said to Jacob, 'Arise, go up to Bethel and dwell there; and make an altar there to God, who appeared to you when you fled from the face of Esau your brother.' And Jacob said to his household and to all who were with him, 'Put away the foreign gods that are among you, purify yourselves, and change your garments. Then let us arise and go up to Bethel; and I will make an altar there to God, who answered me in the

*day of my distress and has been with me in the way which I
have gone.' So they gave Jacob all the foreign gods which were in
their hands, and the earrings which were in their ears; and
Jacob hid them under the terebinth tree which was by Shechem.
And they journeyed...." (Genesis 35:1-5)*

It was a turning point in the patriarch's life. He heard God's
call to "come home," to turn his face back to Bethel, "the
house of God," to return to a place of revelation and commitment. He remembered how the Lord had met with him in a
period of great fear and distress. Before he set out, he got rid of
those things in his life and household that were unholy,
unworthy, and displeasing to the Lord, burying them under a
tree. Arriving at Bethel, he built an altar and worshiped the
Lord with all his heart.

God's call, I believe, is on our lives as well.

The Holy Spirit calls us back to that place where we first
committed our heart to the Lord Jesus...He calls us back to our
"first love" for Him...He calls us to "come home for Christmas."

That "home" is called Calvary—the cross. It's the tree
where the gift of eternal life is given to us. But it is also, like
Jacob's tree, the place where we need to bury everything that is
unworthy—everything that would hinder our forward jour-
ney in God's high purpose for each one of us.

With that understanding in mind, let me invite you to use

your Christmas tree as such a place of recommitment, renewal, or rededication. At some point soon, during these hectic days prior to December 25, take time for your own soul to quietly, humbly "come home." Go alone and kneel—bowing before Jesus at the foot of your Christmas tree or some place of your choosing. Be renewed by the Holy Spirit—the real "Spirit of Christmas." Be released, burying any weights that slow you down, ensnare your soul, or keep your feet from Christmas's joyous, childlike dance or praise in God's presence.

Let's set our face toward Jesus, and as we gather our household around the tree, seek again His lordship and leadership for the coming year.

Making the holidays *holy-days* is the sure path to making them happy days! As our celebration includes rededication, there comes an incredible liberation of joy. Just as Jacob moved on to his God-appointed destiny, relieved from the accumulations of the past, so may we.

Gather at the tree in holy ways, and you'll find the tree the center of the happiest of days!

Hallelujah! He has come!

Gather Round The Tree

Gather 'round the tree and dance with me,
For Christmastime is here,
That lovely time of yearly joying.
Like a little child allow your heart to
Sing, and you will start
to dance around the tree.

Gather in the kitchen for we're fixin'
Bowls and bowls of goodies
Eggnog and hot chocolate beckon.
Here's an empty fudge pan for your lickin'
While your toes are kickin'
dancing 'round the tree.

Gather at the tree and tell the story
Where this Yuletide glory
With its fun and feasting comes from.
Nothing short of God could give us creatures
Anything that features
Such a happy time.

Gather 'round the tree and praise the Savior
  He Who brought the favor
    of the Father's grace and power.
Singing in the glory of such kindness;
  No surprise to find us
  Dancing 'round the tree.

Dancing 'round the tree with happy praises.
  Christmastime brings days of
    happy jubilee.
So come, and
  Gather 'round the tree with me.

A Quiet Corner of Celebration

- Lengthen the value of busy minutes during these busiest days by giving someone the gift of your time.

- Learn the release true humility brings by cracking open a package of personal pride and pouring it out.

- Inconvenience yourself for the sake of someone whose last dream would be your personal interest in them.

- Shock a neighbor with a genuinely warm greeting, accompanied by a simple gift.

- Walk up to a harried store clerk and simply tell her she's doing a good job.

- Give a gas station attendant a tip (whoever heard of that?), and do it in the name of the Christ Child.

- Write some gentle words of compassion to someone you know who is experiencing deep heartaches or trials.

- Drop by a convalescent home and visit two or three rooms. Since you can't see your own folks this Christmas, give love to someone else's.

- Risk the loss of privacy at your treeside and discover the warmth of an enlarged family by inviting someone who isn't related—or even very well known—and providing them with presents, too.

- Help serve at a mission on Christmas Day.

• Phone a friend with whom relationship
has been strained and bear all the responsibility yourself for
the misunderstanding.

• Send flowers to a former school teacher.

• Clear your closets and shelves of unneeded supplies and give
them for distribution through a charitable agency.

• Spend an hour on Christmas
just praying your way around the world.

"For God so loved the world He gave..."

That's the founding of Christmas. Finding it works
the same way.

EXPECTATION

✧

Saints before the altar bending,
Watching long in hope and fear,
Suddenly the Lord, descending,
In His temple shall appear.
Come and worship,
come and worship,
Worship Christ,
the new-born King.

It was Horace Greeley,
the renowned journalist,
who a century ago implored the youthful to turn
their eyes westward if they were seeking opportunity
and great possibilities.
His words, "Go west, young man," still echo today.
The whole flow of civilization's history has
predominantly been westward.

Could that be the Lord's voice I hear . . .
summoning you and me to prepare for
expanded horizons?

We stand together on the brink
of a new year with a sense of anticipation.
Let's "go west," friends in Christ.
Let's open in faith to the new horizons
of opportunity the Lord is bringing into our lives.
You obey in your life, I'll obey in mine,
and together let's possess the wide,
new land of God's high purpose for us all.

He Shall Be Great...Therefore

> *"The Mighty One*
> *has done great things for me—*
> *holy is His name."*
>
> LUKE 1:49, NIV

he echo of the angelic announcement concerning Jesus rings in our ears: "He shall be GREAT and shall be called the Son of the Highest!"

By virtue of the inescapable GREATNESS of our Savior, a resounding "therefore" rises from my lips today.

We have a GREAT SAVIOR

...*Therefore* we are possessors of a *great* salvation, which encompasses every dimension of human need and deserves to be broadcast to every circle where people hurt.

...*Therefore* we are encouraged to expect *great* victories, knowing that great battles are necessary for conquest, but confident because He is leading us.

These two "therefores" provide a focus I ask you to share with me today and into this whole coming year.

The first has to do with our *faith* as believers—moving forward in prayer, intercession, and giving, because the possessing of possibilities requires it.

The second has to do with our *reach* as believers—extending ourselves to touch others, because He has so mightily touched us with His grace and goodness.

Let the new year be a year of growth and harvest!

—Growing in our walk with Jesus—staying close to Him.

—Growing in the Word of God—deepening in understanding.

—Growing in faith, prayer, and boldness in giving.

—Growing in loving, serving, and helping those we can. And,

—Reaching out by every means to touch our community.

—Touching the lost in the confidence His power will save.

—Caring for people who long for someone who will.

—Showing the love of Jesus in ways which gain us the right to be heard, so we can tell of His salvation.

Walk with me and think with me over this thought: There is *nothing* too great for us to expect since we have *so great* a Savior and Lord.

Sing That Name to Me

Sing that Name to me in sweetest harmony.
Whisper tenderly the Name of Jesus—Jesus, Jesus.
Sing that Name, praise the Name of Jesus Christ the Lord.

Captives are set free and souls at liberty,
Darkness made to flee when you sing Jesus—Jesus, Jesus.
Now we raise songs of praise to Jesus Christ the Lord.

> *The honor and glory belong unto Thee,*
> *The wisdom and power and all majesty.*
> *In worship extolling Thy full victory*
> *We exalt in praise the wondrous Name of Jesus.*

Bodies may be healed, hearts are made to yield,
Glory is revealed when we sing Jesus—Jesus, Jesus.
Now we sing praise to our King, Jesus Christ the Lord.

Unraveling Snafus

*If it is possible, as much as depends
on you, live peaceably with all men.*
ROMANS 12:18

hen normally fallible human beings become very busy and preoccupied, their fallibility quotient rises dramatically. And is there any time of year when we become more busy and preoccupied than in the days just before Christmas?

Maybe that explains how one of my relationships became so tangled, snarled, and jumbled just recently. So...along with writing Christmas cards and notes, I also found myself writing a letter of explanation.

"I'm writing," I began, "to attempt somehow to clear up the confusion that surrounded our recent exchange of notes, calls, attempts at contact, etc."

My letter went on to interpret what had happened. I hoped it would help, but I didn't expect a cure. Hindsight explanations don't usually seem adequate to unravel the mind-boggling tangles two fallible humans seem capable of at times.

In World War II, the military coined an acronym for it—SNAFU: Situation Normal, All Fouled Up. That's another way of saying, "Wherever people are involved, let's simply adapt ourselves to the necessity of things being messed up."

But that kind of "normalcy" isn't tolerable—especially in relationships. Too many snares snag at the soul already, tearing joy and meaning from our lives. I vote for confronting them all—and I assert that strained, wounded, or broken relationships are primary points of beginning if we are to be truly free.

What to do?

As with my letter, I suggest the following where relationships have been "snafued." Contact—by letter, phone, or in person—might include the following elements:

Affirm your deep sense of value for the person involved.

All of us need to be needed. All of us are threatened with a sense of limited worth. All of us feel misunderstood. All of us need bolstering. It isn't a matter of pampering or babying; it's simply a matter of needing to be cared about.

Request the other person's understanding of your own ineptness or failure.

You and I are in a stronger position when we acknowledge our helplessness, weakness, and dependence upon the patience of others. In doing so I am not asking people for permission to act and remain careless or immature. Not at all. But I am saying that my humanity makes for a lot of cracks in my perfection. Rather than building a facade, we need help from patient people in patching up the cracks in the plaster of our personalities. Let's ask for that help.

Be patient yourself, if your overtures don't receive an immediate response.

Our finest attempts have a way of bouncing back in our faces at times. But believe me, the Holy Spirit can bless the spirit of your approach even beyond what your words can do. The fact of your attempt provides grounds for His ongoing working.

Don't succumb to the flesh-thought, *I'd better leave well enough alone.* "Snafu" isn't "well enough." Who wants to slog into the new year knee-deep in snafus? Unraveling, like a child's spaghettied shoelaces, often takes time and patience.

Join me, won't you? With our Lord's help, SNAFU *could* mean, "Situation Normal, All *Fixed* Up."

THE "LOST" WEEK OF THE YEAR

See that you walk circumspectly,
not as fools but as wise, redeeming the time,
because the days are evil.

EPHESIANS 5:15-16

he *last* week of each year tends to become the *lost* week.

Have you noticed? Once we turn the corner of Christmas, everything blurs. From December 26 to January 2 we slip into a state of "hyper-holiday suspended animation." As far as truly fruitful living is concerned, we might as well have spent the week on Mars.

I've prepared a list of suggested activities to allow you to keep enjoying the spirit of the holidays, while still making solid use of those transitional days. Lord willing, these suggestions will help keep the blur out and the focus in! This week—call it "Countdown Week" as we approach the New Year—you might give a day or a part of one to any or all of the following.

1. Fast and pray.

Skip a meal (or two or three) and seek the Lord. This isn't a "religious" exercise, it's a realistic one. It prioritizes seeking His face, observes a proven, powerful, spiritual discipline and (for some of us) breaks the "feast" routine of the season. Give your body, soul, and spirit a break!

2. Read a large book in the Bible.

Get a running start on your goal of reading through the Word in the new year. It takes about three to four minutes to thoroughly read an average page in the Bible. Take two to four hours and read a Bible book all the way through. Genesis covers sixty-three pages in my Bible (about three to four hours) and Revelation's twenty-one chapters (about an hour and a half). Pick your own size book, take an evening or afternoon, and feast there!

3. Undress the house.

Many of us celebrate Christmas with festive decor and few (if any) surpass what Anna does at our place! Some years ago we learned the wisdom (at least for us!) of getting the Christmas dressings "undressed" by New Year's Day. It puts a fresh face on everything and emotionally gears you to walk into the year without feeling you're already behind—still trying to finish off the old one.

4. Send thank-you notes and letters.

Don't be forgetful of a commonly neglected but much-appreciated practice. The briefest note of thanks or letter of warmth and love at this season speaks volumes! Take the time necessary. Let people know you appreciate them…and their gift, too.

5. Set aside time for "fullness."

As appropriate as holiday celebration is, it's very natural to find yourself drained by all the action and activity. A dullness or listless apathy may besiege the soul at this time of year, unless…*unless* we seek the Lord for a refreshing and refilling of His Spirit.

6. Summarize…organize.

Loose ends tend to fly in the breeze as year-end winds blow. Take a couple hours, sit down with a notebook, and ask the Lord to help you think of things which need to be tabulated for future action. Pay special attention to those nagging, left-over, still-to-do things from last year's list. Who wants to drag a cloud of unease and uncertainty into the bright, fresh days of the new year? Zeroing in on these long-neglected items can help blow the fog away as you step over the threshold of January 1. No, we will *never* get everything done. But somehow, just knowing what is left and listing it on paper gives a sense of completion and closure. It's an act that removes guilt and opens the way to positive action.

Don't wander down from a bright Christmas mountaintop into a swamp of indecision, lethargy, and wasted opportunity. When that first Christmas was over, Joseph heard the words of the Lord's angel and took immediate action, saving the life of the Child.

That's what I want to do: Listen for His voice and then do what He says without doubt or procrastination. There's no telling how far you might go this year with that kind of head start!

The Upward Call

Hear the Upward call of the Master;
Lift your eyes and you will see
New horizons appear,
and the challenge is clear,
Come and climb the heights with me.

Never let your heart be shackled
by affections earthly bound.
Follow Christ today
up the narrow way
That leads to higher ground.

STARTING OVER

When those bitter days
have come upon you in the latter times,
you will finally return to the Lord your God
and listen to what He tells you.

DEUTERONOMY 4:30, TLB

I hear a loud, clear call of the Spirit these days: "Repent and do the first works" (Revelation 2:5).

It resounds from the heart of Jesus and summons from the written Word of God. It is a herald to us as we prepare for the opening weeks of a new year.

We are standing on holy ground. By any measure or estimate, we have come through a cycle of years. I can put my finger on a number of such cycles:

...The years since Anna and I received our call to ministry.

...The years since we began our service here at The Church On The Way.

...The years since our congregation received a special intercessory assignment from the Lord.

You supply your own numbers and milestones. How many years

...Since you surrendered to Jesus as Lord of your life?

...Since you stood with your life partner and repeated vows of marriage before the Lord?

...Since His Spirit led you into the church where you find fellowship?

...Since you turned your back on some besetting sin?

...Since you submitted to the Spirit's call for a special area of service?

That cycle of years is, I am convinced by the Lord, intended to bring us to a place of starting over. Please note that I said *starting over*. I did not say *beginning again*.

Is there a difference? Oh, yes.

To *start over* is to return to your roots and nourish them. It is to assure yourself that you remember what it is that makes you tick.

For senators and congressional representatives, it's getting back to their home states and districts, walking the streets, neighborhoods, boroughs, parishes, and precincts. It's sipping coffee with citizens in the diners and lunchrooms. It's getting behind the mike on local radio call-in programs and holding town meetings.

For professional athletes, it's participating in off-season camps and clinics and drills that reemphasize the fundamentals of the game.

For Monopoly buffs, it's returning to "GO" and, best of all, "collecting $200!"

Starting over doesn't involve loss, but it does require humility. And that has an assured reward.

Beginning again, on the other hand, is what you do when a tornado destroys the farm. When a storm washes away the bridge. When an earthquake rips the house off its foundation. When moral failure poisons the purity of trust in a relationship.

The Lord, who calls us to return to those things which His Word teaches and which release the power of His presence among us, is not making a statement about anything being so lost, ruined, or wrecked that there is nothing of spiritual capital with which to start afresh.

But He is saying that our assignment is to become as children all over again.

To kneel again at the altar of our first commitment.

To return to our first love.

To perform our first works.

So renewed, we will be mightily released unto His highest purpose and praise.

A Personal Note

His birth began an ever-expanding family…
"For God so loved the world…"
begins the most precious verse in the Bible.
"That He gave His only begotten Son"
describes the most incredible love known to mankind.

And because of that love, at this beloved season,
we celebrate the ever-expanding family of God—
the continuously growing Body of Christ, redeemed to new
birth through the Lamb born in Bethlehem's stall.

My wife, Anna, and I are glad you're part of that family
with us! And our still-expanding Hayford family sends its love
and joyous greetings to you—this Christmas,
this New Year, and always…until He comes again.
Christmas says, "Come and behold Him."
A New Year shouts, "Go forth…and live in His love,
power, and great joy!"

Jack and Anna Hayford

Notes